D1740843

SAVED BY TENNIS

Retirement and Ageing

By
Lawrence Greene

ISBN-13: 978-1502892140
ISBN-10: 1502892146

Cover art by Joleene Naylor - All rights reserved

Manufactured/Produced in the United States

CONTENTS

ACKNOWLEDGEMENTS

I would like to thank my local Lawn Tennis Club (the Club), its coaching staff and administration for the many positive experiences that I have had as a member over the past three years. I would particularly like to thank the coaching staff and members of the Monday morning Over-45s group for providing the setting and encouragement that enabled me to get launched in my tennis career. Special thanks also for Mike and for Sam for being my early partners in singles friendlies and to the 'tennis ladies' for ushering me into the world of doubles. Tim's patience with me in our individual coaching sessions is also greatly appreciated and I hope to someday be able to emulate the play of his many 12-year-old prodigies!

PREFACE

This book is essentially the story of how I took up tennis as a 70-year-old. It also relates how I was faced with a plethora of free time when I retired and how I dealt with that challenge. Writing about the issue of free time led me to think more widely on the subject and to offer some cautionary advice to people who are approaching their retirement years.

I am in no way an expert on tennis and I have not read any books about playing tennis nor have I done any research on tennis before penning this work. It is a personal memoir based on my experience as a rank amateur. To that end, I offer my sincere apologies if I have made any technical errors of fact in describing the game of tennis. The strategies that I developed are merely my own and are not based on formal instruction.

I began playing tennis without any previous experience when I was 70-years-of-age by joining a local Lawn Tennis Club in the city in England in which I live and by participating in a beginner's class. My experiences in playing tennis are almost entirely based on my experiences at the Club over the past three years. Although there is nothing personal in this account, I have chosen to leave the name and location of the Club anonymous. I have used fictitious names in referring to people who are part of this story and I have been careful not to say anything judgemental about any of the characters in the memoir. However, I do apologise to the coaching staff at the Club for any errors that I may have made in conveying some of the content of formal coaching sessions. And, I apologise to the administration of the Club for any errors that I may have made in describing the physical layout of the courts or the organisation of the Club.

I am not a retirement counsellor, so any advice that I have given about preparation for retirement is merely based on my own experience and is not informed by any research, training or certification.

I have had to convey to the reader some amount of information about my life history in order to provide the context for understanding what led me to take up tennis as a 70-year-old. I have tried to keep the detail to a minimum, but yet leave enough there so that the reader would still have some sense of me as a person and of my particular needs at that point of time in my life. I apologise to my family if I have said anything that they feel is unnecessary.

Finally, some of my concerns about making line calls may seem unusual to people who have been playing tennis all of their lives, but weighed heavily on me at the time as everything about the game was simultaneously new.

Lawrence Greene

Figure 1 Standard Tennis Court

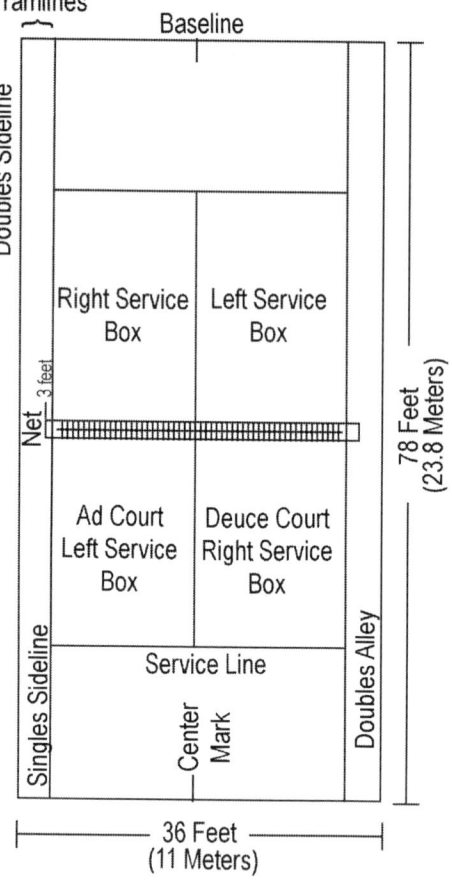

CHAPTER ONE

Retirement And Ageing

Retirement

I wouldn't say that my life has actually been saved by tennis in that I would have died if I had not played tennis. What I mean is that the quality of my life has been saved by tennis, and that I probably would have been a somewhat depressed person if I hadn't stumbled upon tennis. And, I am not saying that tennis is the salvation for everyone, that it could solve everyone's problems and certainly not the world's problems. I only am saying that it worked for me, that it helped me solve a part of my problem – that problem being what does one do when one retires when you are in your 60s and you are confronted with the fact that you have a huge amount of time on your hands, and when you are simultaneously confronted by the fact that you are an older person and that the process of ageing has had an impact on your physical and mental abilities and that you are no longer quite the person you thought you were when you were in your 30s, or 40s, or even in your 50s?

This work is a love letter to tennis in that tennis helped keep me from sliding into a somewhat dark place. But, again, it is merely one of many pursuits which can serve the same purpose. It is a matter of finding what works for you. Jogging did it for me for many years until I suffered from a compressed spinal nerve in my lower back and subsequent spinal surgery when I was 70, requiring that I give up what had been an important form of relaxation for me as well as an important means of validation of my sense of well-being and relative youth. Hiking, rambling, and mountain climbing work for many people, and there are innumerable rambling groups that are primarily made up of retired people and which provide varying degrees of exercise as well as the conviviality of a group that may enjoy a pub lunch after their weekly ramble.

Or, you can collect antiques, or stamps, or works of art, or take up playing competitive chess, or join a cycling group, or become a member of a dance group, or play golf, or play bridge, or join a theatre group or just frequent the theatre or ballet or art museums on your own, or travel extensively, or make a serious stab at becoming a gourmet chef, or become involved with a charity, or join a choir or orchestra, or learn a foreign language, or take courses. Or whatever! All of these activities, among others, are enriching throughout our lives and we all engage in a number of them to different degrees during our working lives.

But, in retirement things change completely. One moves, sometimes very quickly and unexpectedly, from a situation in which your life is highly structured by the requirements of your work obligations and where there is frequently relatively little additional time in your life for avocations beyond work, house, and children, to a situation in which there are absolutely no obligations associated with employment and simultaneously one's involvement in the daily lives of your now grown children may have become minimal at most.

Although this book started out as a straightforward love letter to tennis, in the process of writing it also has morphed into a cautionary tale about retirement for I have come to see that our avocations or hobbies take on a much greater valency in our lives when one has retired and when you must simultaneously confront both the greatest blessing and most profound challenge of retirement – a plethora of free time.

People move into retirement in different ways and with different needs. Some people slowly transition out of satisfying work situations into working a reduced number of hours when they are in their 60s and eventually retire in their mid-to-late 60s. Similarly, others might take early retirement in their early 60s and then continue to work in a satisfying work situation with post-retirement part-time employment for two or three or four years. In both cases this leads to a situation where there is only an incremental increase in one's free time and a continued connection to the structuring of one's life that is provided by employment.

Others of us move into retirement much more rapidly and with, perhaps, a bit less planning. Some people of retireable age in their late 50s or early 60s are forced into retirement by redundancy and with limited or no possibility of employment, while others in somewhat unsatisfactory work situations are tempted into retirement by attractive, but unexpected, system-wide early retirement offers that come out of the blue. Both of these groups may find that they are fully retired from employment and are relatively well-off financially, but may now face a life in which they have vast amounts of time on their hands and somewhat limited ways of making use of that time.

Many people begin to travel more when they retire, but continuous travelling can be both expensive and tiring, unless, I suppose, you purchase a caravan and do your traveling on the cheap. But, there is only so much traveling one can do, especially if you have a family home that you wish to maintain. Therefore, it begins to become important to have other things to do – beyond a trip once or twice or three times a year – if you find that you are relatively sedentary due to: financial factors; health reasons for yourself or your partner; a need to occupy and maintain your home and property; or family obligations.

For those of us who have acquired a number of avocations or hobbies in the course of our lives the move into retirement and the free time that it provides may be cushioned to a considerable degree. If you already play golf you can play more golf and if you are a keen gardener you can spend that much more time in the garden or embark on more ambitious gardening projects. If you are a chess player or a bridge player you will have more time for chess or for bridge. If you enjoy hiking or rambling you can do more hiking or you can join a rambling group and do more and lengthier rambles. If you already play an instrument in an amateur orchestra, in retirement you can join a second orchestra or a chamber group. If you already do volunteer work for a charity, in retirement you can increase the amount of time you spend working for that charity or you can do additional volunteer work for another charity. And if, unfortunately or fortunately as the case may be, you have children and grandchildren and if you help with grandchild care, in retirement you can help out that much more if you are so inclined. Therefore, whatever avocations or activities that you engage in during your years of employment can be continued or expanded during retirement and thus serve as pleasant ways of utilising your time.

However, what about those of us who, for whatever reasons, have not had many avocations or hobbies during our working lives, and those of us who do not have children or grandchildren nearby or who are not particularly inclined to throw ourselves into routine grandchild care obligations for five or ten years? How do people from this second group, who precipitously move into retirement without a bagful of avocations and interests in place, deal with the challenge of doing something useful and fulfilling with our time beyond sleeping late and watching television? You will probably find that some normal every day activities become prolonged when you are retired and just take up more time. You may not sleep much later, but you might take a bit more time getting out of bed and may listen to the radio a bit more and you may have a somewhat more leisurely breakfast. And you may find that you spend a bit more time communicating with your family and friends by email or text or telephone/skype. And you probably will find that you spend a bit more time doing food shopping rather than rushedly picking up a few things on the way home from work. And you may spend more time on cooking and may become somewhat more adventurous in the process. And you will certainly travel more frequently and take some longer holidays to more far-off places, within the limits of your ability to afford such trips.

However, at the end of the day you still will have wads of time on your hands. If you take three or four two-to-three week-long trips each year there still will be nine or ten months of the year when you are home. And you just can't linger over breakfast all day or chat on the telephone or email or text your family and mates all day! And shopping, hopefully, is only once a week and cleaning, even more hopefully, is only a nonce-a-week activity or a once-a-week activity if you have a cleaner. So, what will you do with your time?

The answer for those of us who have had a number or avocations and interests throughout our working lives is to devote more time to those avocations and interests in our retirement. But what about those of us who, for whatever reasons, have had few avocations and interests during our working lives – possibly because we devoted an excessive amount of time and energy to our jobs or children or whatever? The obvious answer here is for those of us who find ourselves in this position to develop new interests or hobbies or avocations! Take up golf or tennis or cycling. Go hiking or join a rambling group. Take up chess or learn a new foreign language or improve your speaking skills in a foreign language you already know. Get into gardening. Join a choir or an orchestra. Join a theatre group. Volunteer at a charity, or a hospital, or a residential home for the elderly, or at the Citizens' Advice Bureau. Or, do some extensive home renovation that you always wanted to do, like building a conservatory.

Besides complex DIY building projects, none of

these activities are exactly like rocket science. All of us could get involved in some of these endeavours. Picking up chess or learning a foreign language may not be for every one and you have to be inclined to physical activity if you want to take up tennis or cycling with a somewhat serious level of commitment. But, golf, hiking and swimming are very accessible sports and gardening is an option for virtually everyone. And, there are innumerable secular and religious charities that have a great need for volunteers. Or, you can get involved in local politics and local government.

All of these activities are doable. It is just a matter of getting it together to do it. Yet, that can be more problematic if you enter retirement with no or few avocations and you suddenly find yourself striking out in several new directions because you have the time to do so. There is a lot of learning involved if you decide to pick-up tennis, or golf, or bridge, or chess, or a foreign language from scratch. It is much more difficult to fill up your time in retirement by learning something new, or several new things, compared to expanding the time you spend on an activity that you already know. In the following chapters I will tell you about the challenge I faced in taking up tennis, a game that was entirely new to me, as my principal sport and my principal avocation in the 70th year of my life. Taking up one or two or three entirely new avocations or interests in one's retirement requires a considerable amount of work and learning and is a much more difficult process than expanding upon activities with which you are already familiar and which you have mastered over the years. It can be a bit of a jolt to the system, or to one's ego, in the first year or so of retirement if you move from a position as an experienced senior member of a work group into a position in retirement where, because you are looking for ways to fill up your time, you are in multiple novice learning roles in new activities, e.g., as a novice chess player, and a completely novice tennis player, and as a member of a foreign language conversation class that is a bit over your head, and as a volunteer in a charity activity that is entirely new to you and which is somewhat technically challenging or challenging from a managerial perspective.

Therefore, if you are all-consumed with work and find that you have no avocations or non-work-related interests, it may be a good strategy to take up an avocation or hobby or interest while you are younger and still at work so that they will be available to you in at least half-ready form when you are fully retired and are searching for things to do.

Ageing

I should also say something about ageing, the effects of which tend to kick in around the time we retire and which provides an additional challenge for us during the period of our retirement. A sad irony about the process of retirement is that it tends to come around the time that we are just beginning to feel, or be aware of, the effects of ageing on our physical and mental well-being. I was hospitalised with a serious neck injury in an auto accident at age 25, but subsequent to that time I was never a patient in a hospital until about the 65th year of my life and rarely saw my general practice doctor except for very routine and inconsequential medical issues. And it was the same with my wife Jenny. However, once we hit our mid-60s the effects of ageing set in and visits to our medical practice and local hospital became a routine part of our lives. Nothing especially crippling, but enough to slow us down somewhat – arthritis, knee problems and irritable bowel for Jenny and an arthritic big toe (gout?), back problems and benign prostate enlargement for me. And, I certainly do not jog at anywhere near the speed that I used to run and I also cycle more slowly than the 30 and 40 and 50-year-olds. Furthermore, when I started to play tennis I was absolutely shocked to find that I could no longer throw a tennis ball with anywhere near the ease that I did in my youth! With respect to our mental capacities, I am happy to report that they are still largely intact and that Jenny remembers the name and relation of every person that is mentioned in any conversation, although she cannot remember her own mobile/cell telephone number, and that she is an ace at the crossword puzzles and has perfect hearing, while my capabilities in these areas are merely adequate. However, I do notice that we tend to be good at the things that we always were good at, while somewhat less impressive at learning entirely new things – like getting the full benefit from our mobile/cell phones!

Thus, the cautionary tale is that it is a lot more difficult to learn a completely new avocation/hobby in your retirement when you are older, say in your 60s or 70s. It is not impossible, but it just comes somewhat more slowly. This certainly has been my experience with tennis and many, or most people, have some difficulty learning a new foreign language late in life if they are not a linguist or a person who is particularly linguistically gifted. Therefore, if you want to be systematic in your preparation for retirement do try to have two or three avocations under your belt by the time you retire so that you will not find yourself in the position of having a vast amount of time on your hands but are intimidated from learning anything new by the discomfort of being a complete novice in a number of endeavours where most other participants in these activities are much more accomplished than you.

CHAPTER TWO

Early Days In Tennis

I was an academic and retired when I was 62-years-old and found myself with a considerable amount of time on my hands. I had been a regular, but not competitive, jogger, but a compressed spinal nerve in the lumbar region of my back when I was 70, and subsequent spinal surgery, put an end to anything more than an occasional 30-minute run on the track at the University's sports complex. My surgeon suggested that I take up Pilates to strengthen my core muscles and surprisingly told me that I could play tennis as well, given that it did not entail the constant pounding of jogging. Therefore, in the 70th year of my life I found myself turning to tennis as my main form of physical exercise. I had actually never played a game, or match, of tennis in my life, although for many years I had a wooden tennis racket and would on rare occasions hit a ball against a tennis practice wall. The first time that I actually hit a tennis ball on a court was, I believe, in about 1974 when I was 34-years-of age and was at a week-long nutrition conference during the summer. I must have bought a racket specifically for the occasion and I vaguely remember hitting the ball back and forth with a colleague, mainly using forehand strokes. Subsequently, I lived for 24 years in a community that had three excellent tennis courts. But, I never

ever played a single game of tennis during that period of time, except to very occasionally hit the ball against the practice wall, and only two or three times rally with two of my sons for no more than about an hour. I just did not have the time to play tennis. It seemed bourgeois, something that serious people did not do, and as far as I knew none of my colleagues played. I believe that the only time that I played a bit more was during a sabbatical in England in 1991/92 when I hit it around with my 14-year-old son Jeremy two or three times on the grass courts at one of the colleges. But, I had never played a game, or a match, and although I had occasionally watched the Wimbledon or the French Open tennis competition on television in Britain after I had retired I still really did not know the basic format and rules of the game besides the fact that the one player served and the two players hit the ball back and forth until one failed to keep the ball on the court.

Beginner's Class

In February 2012 I joined a local tennis club for the over-the-age-of-70 fee of £203 (about $315) per year and enrolled in a beginner's class that met for one-and-a-half hours once a week. There were about 15 members in the class and they were all much younger than I, mostly in their 20s and 30s. One of the first things that I remember about the Beginner's Class was that when we did the various legwork exercises at the start of the class I was one of the slowest and least adept of the participants. I consider myself to be very athletic and was more than a bit shocked as most of the members of the class were not very athletic looking women in their 20s! Although not a tennis player, I had jogged all of my life and in my youth in the U.S., to about age 18, I had played basketball and some form of baseball almost daily.

I was 70-years-of-age, but had an image of myself as being rather youthful and quite fit. Although I was usually passed (exceeded in speed) by other joggers during my solitary morning jogs, I attributed that to the fact that I was probably running a longer distance than they were and I felt that I could have increased my speed if I desired to do so.

Seeing myself struggle relative to my classmates in these legwork stepping exercises made me aware, rather harshly, of the fact that I am an older person and that my level of physical fitness is not what I had thought it to be. This was made dramatically clearer to me when the coach asked us to throw a tennis ball across the width of the three courts. As a former baseball player and sometimes pitcher I vividly remember myself whipping a baseball or softball or pink stick ball around with ease and abandon. And, I could remember still doing that with my son Jeremy when he was about 13-years-old and I was about 50. So, it was with complete shock and dismay to find that I had absolutely no arm strength at all and that I could barely launch the ball across the width of two courts! All of the familiarity of throwing a ball seemed to have been lost. All of the neuromotor memory was just gone. And it became shockingly clear that I am now an older person and that many of my physical capabilities are now gone, or greatly diminished.

I remembered that during the last few years of

work as an academic I had noticed that it was becoming difficult to reach up on the blackboard to write and that I had lowered the point at which I began writing to a more middle level of the backboard. At that time I had wondered whether my right shoulder was becoming stiff, but had convinced myself that it was mainly the rather heavy and stiff tweed jackets that I tended to wear that was impeding my shoulder movement. But I now saw that it was me, and not my tweed jackets, that lacked normal shoulder movement and which now lacked the arm strength and neuromuscular fluidity that I remembered from my youth. Instead of this ease and fluidity, my arm movement lacked strength and my leg movement seemed relatively rigid compared to my nimble darting about as a youthful basketball player.

I was thus very quickly and harshly alerted to the fact that old age had set in, and that if the very familiar throw of the ball of my youth was now something that I could barely do, the less familiar swing of the tennis racket, particularly my backhand swing, would really be something that I would be learning *de novo* and with reduced neuromuscular capabilities, and that it is not something that is there and just has to be retrieved and polished a bit.

This was quite a surprise because I had taken to riding a bicycle again without any problems when I relocated to England in my early 60s. I had ridden a cycle in my youth, but cannot remember having ridden as an adult except one weekend that I had spent in Nantucket when I was in my 40s. However, I did have a cycle when I spent a sabbatical year in England in my early 50s and did ride from college to work quite regularly. I suppose that I had been able to re-establish the neuromuscular wiring associated with cycle riding during middle age and did not have to try to take up cycling again in my 70s without that experience.

But, bicycle riding skills seems to be something that one learns quite early, if one learns it at all, and that one usually employs them constantly over many years in one's youth. So if you stop riding when you are 16 or 18 or whatever age, you already have many years of practice under your belt. Tennis is different. If you have just hit it around a bit when you were younger and then only taken it up again when you are 70 there is just not the same level of neuromuscular memory to draw upon. It is really a matter of starting from scratch. A comparison with the acquisition of a foreign language seems appropriate. Someone who learns to speak a foreign language well in their youth and then does not use it again until much later in life is likely to find the task of learning, or relearning, the language to be far easier than the person who in his/her 60s or 70s first tries to learn the language.

So, the first thing that I was confronted with was that I was a relatively old man who was trying to begin playing a new sport while equipped with a rather broken down old body that had little or no neuromuscular memory in my arms and legs of the movements utilised in that sport. And, I was trying to learn how to play this game not in the privacy of individual lessons or on a private court, but in a group setting with a bunch of limber youths a third of my age.

Another problem that I had in trying to learn an almost completely new sport in my 70s was the transition that I had to make from being the one who was the teacher or lecturer to one who is a learner or novice. A further problem was being in a class with a group of people who were from half to a third of my age! When you are an academic you become accustomed to being in the role of the expert and having the status associated with that role. Here, I found myself in the role of the complete novice who lacked the physical skills to play the game well and who simultaneously had only a cursory knowledge of the rules of the game, let alone any idea of the basic strategies employed in the game.

Basics

As a 70-year-old I would not say that I was a fast learner. Despite being instructed on the forehand grip and the single-handed backhand grip and the chopper grip for volleying, I found that my hand just tended to slide back into a comfortable forehand grip irrespective of the requirements of the return. And there seemed to be so many other things to be thinking of, particularly my leg work and where I intended to return the ball on my opponent's side of the court. I soon learned that a nice straight medium-speed return straight down the middle of the court would likely lead to, with any decent opponent, a rather strong forehand return deep to my rather weak backhand. So, the placement and speed of my returns quickly assumed considerable significance.

I eventually developed a decent ground game over the almost two-and-a-half years that I have been playing, but I would not say that I am particularly good. Developing a strong serve is something that seems to have eluded me, much to my surprise. Being a former ardent baseball player, I thought that serving would be a bit like pitching and that it would come easily. Unfortunately, that has not been the case. My serve is somewhat satisfactory, but it lacks the speed necessary to create much of an advantage for myself. A slow-to-moderately paced serve, even if well-placed, to a capable opponent is likely to come flying back at speed and probably to my backhand.

Why I cannot get as much speed as I would like into my serve is one of the main mysteries of the game to me and one of the tennis projects that I am devoting myself to during the coming winter season. I was in an auto accident when I was 25-years-old when a lady friend who was driving my car managed to lose control and turn it over with me inside, the consequence of which is that I sustained a serious neck injury and had a spinal fusion between my third and fourth cervical vertebrae. The surgery was successful and I have not had any pain over the years, but I have some limitation in extending my neck – bending it back – which makes it a bit difficult for me to throw the ball up high when I serve, rise up with my head bent back, and hit the ball at the crest of my throw. It is just not something that I can comfortably do! Instead, I tend to throw the ball up a rather short distance and probably hit it at about two o'clock rather than at twelve o'clock. And, as of the moment, I don't get up on my toes enough to get any contribution from my legs in my serve. I'm really not certain what the correct way is to do it, but I am certain that I am not doing it whatever it may be. My serves tend to have modest pace and come in quite low, but lack enough velocity to give me that much advantage when I serve.

The Beginner's Course provided me with a brief introduction to tennis. I'm embarrassed to say that after living what I would call an upper middle class life and at 70-years-of-age I didn't know the basic rules and vocabulary of tennis as I had never really played a game. Baseline, service line, tram lines, volley, slam, rally, correct scoring, tie breaks, etc. were all new to me. And the difference in strategy in singles and doubles was also completely new.

It was like learning a foreign language for the very first time in the 70th year of your life without the benefit of ever having any experience or practice speaking it during one's youth. There were just so many things to do simultaneously: making a call as to whether a serve or return is in or out while you are preparing to hit the ball and are not concentrating on the exact position of the ball relative to the lines; keeping track of the score; changing sides after two games; the speed and placement of your serve and making sure that you don't double fault; anticipating where your opponent's return will be coming and simultaneously deciding where you wish to direct your return, preferably not right up the middle; keeping your returns deep, but with an occasional well-placed drop shot; the direction and speed of the wind; going to the net on serve or thereafter; keeping enough pace on the ball throughout the match; making sure to bend when you hit your return; pacing your 70-year-old self, particularly when you are playing opponents who are 30 to 40 years younger than you; dealing with an opponent who has a very strong first serve, how and where to return it; the format for a tie break, where do you begin serving and remembering to change sides after six points. All of these things going on simultaneously were as challenging to me as trying to respond to a fluent French speaker in perfect French using the subjunctive!

I came out of the first eight-week Beginner's Course with a basic sense of the game of tennis and with some sense of what I should be doing with my forehand and backhand and volley shots and slams. But it was all very preliminary and I didn't feel confident enough to venture onto the club courts outside the protective confines of the Beginner's Course. And, I didn't have anyone with whom I could play! So, I took the Beginner's Course again during the spring. By the time the second eight-week course was finished I felt much more confident about moving onto another level. And, I was particularly anxious to find people with whom I could play singles friendlies. The Beginner's Class was in the evening and all of the participants were younger and worked during the day, so they were not likely singles partners and I was not keen on playing in the evening in the reduced light of the outdoor courts even when they were floodlit.

CHAPTER THREE

Over-45s

I noticed in the club's schedule of courses that there was an Over-45s drop-in session for £5 ($8) on Monday mornings from 9:30 to 11:00. After consulting with the coach of the Beginner's Course I summoned the courage to attend one of these sessions. Most of the participants were in their 50s or early 60s and were much more accomplished players than myself. Many of the 12 to 14 players who came weekly had been playing for years and used the Over-45s session as a way to get some additional practice and instruction. Several had only been playing for three or four years, but no one in the group was a rank novice like me. It was a mixed group, about 60 percent male and 40 percent female, and some of them were fairly decent tennis players who came to this session for social purposes as well as to practice their tennis. But, no one in this group was a really strong player, say someone who would be in the top half of the club's individual rankings.

As I said, there were usually 12 to 14 participants in the Over-45s group and if the weather was foul there might only be eight to ten of us, but rarely fewer than that. Tim, a chap of around 32-years-of-age when I began and one of the four principal coaches at the club, was the coach. He is a terrific tennis player and has been the men's singles champion at the club for most of the past few years. Tim is an easy-going and jolly fellow who maintained good rapport and lots of banter with the group. This, in addition to the practice and coaching that we received, made the Monday mornings Over-45s group a pleasant social event. Although there is a £5 walk-on fee, most of the people who came were regular attendees with new people coming for one or two sessions on occasion.

The Over-45s session runs for 1 ½ hours and was mainly drills and competitions among the participants. I have not made a detailed list of these drills, but the following provides a good overview of the mix of drills and competitions that comprised a typical session. If there were just twelve of us then we would use three adjacent carpeted courts divided in half so that there would be six pairs, or twelve players, on the three courts. If there were more attendees we also would use one or two of the nearby carpeted courts from a separate group of courts.

1. Practicing Volleys and Slams

Volleys

I don't remember us doing this very much in the recent past, but when I first began attending the Over-45s group two years ago we did a fair amount of practice with volleys and slams. Perhaps that was because some of the new regular attendees – like myself, Mike, Sam, and Alice – were relatively new at the game and at that time had only been playing for one or two years. The format for these drills was to pair up with two people on half of the court, one on each side of the net. The person practicing his/her volley would stand three feet beyond the net and his/her partner would be at the baseline on the other side of the net and would hit balls alternatively to the forehand then backhand side of the person who was hitting the volleys. The goal of the exercise is to get ten good volleys returned, preferably between the service line and the baseline (see Figure 1). After one of the pair achieved that goal, they would switch and the server/hitter would do the volleys and vice versa. This was a reasonably useful exercise, but a lot depended on the server/hitter delivering the ball reasonably close to the person hitting the volleys and alternatively to the forehand and then the backhand side.

I wasn't great at these volleying drills, but I was not that bad. However, I was to find out that it was a lot easier to do this in a drill when you knew that the ball was being hit directly to you and at a moderate speed, compared to doing it in a singles or doubles match when you didn't know when the ball would be coming at you and when it could arrive with considerable speed.

Slams

The format for practicing slams was the same as with volleys – in pairs on half of the court with a server/hitter at his/her baseline and the slammer standing about three feet away from the net on the other side of the net. Here, the server would hit a ball underhand so that it would loop up quite high, 20 to 30 feet, and come down between the net and the service line. The slammer would hit this slowly-descending ball as it arrives above his head with a powerful overhand return similar to that which you employ when you serve. A slam opportunity should provide a sure point in a match because the ball is arriving slowly and is usually close to the net and is the result of a defensive return or a poorly executed lob. However, slams are just not my cup of tea. I have a spinal fusion in my neck at C3/C4 that limits the degree to which I can comfortably look up at a lofted ball, just as it hampers me from looking up when I serve, and I am not particularly good at judging the descent of the ball and reliably connecting with it to produce a strong slam onto my opponent's side of the court. It is not a shot that is used all that much during a match, so I am concentrating on my volleying technique and leaving slams to my future development. Whcn I am presented with a slam opportunity on a lob in a match I do take it, but the result, rather than a sure point, is likely to be 50/50!

2. Rallying Drills

As noted, we did some volley drills and slam drills a while ago, but they are not a regular part what we now do in the Over-45s group. We usually begin the session with rallying on half of the court, including the tramlines. We pair up with anyone and just hit it back and forth for five minutes or so until Tim gives us a more structured drill. One such drill is to rally back and forth until we have hit 40 returns between the service line and the baseline. Once that is achieved by one pair we usually would move on to another similar drill such as rallying back and forth with the aim of getting 40 returns within the tramlines (see Figure 1). Both of these are warm-up drills with the goal of getting us to develop better control of the placement of our returns – deeper in the first drill and to the side line in the second.

Sometimes Tim would then follow the above two drills with a doubles rally drill. In this exercise the two players on one side of the net on each court become a team and the two players on the other side of the net form the opposing team. One team begins this competitive exercise with an easy-to-return underhand serve which either member of the opposing team would then return. The following shot would have to be returned by the second member of the team irrespective of where it is hit. The process continues with the members of both teams alternating in making the returns. The purpose of this drill is to prepare us for doubles play by putting us in a situation where we must work as a team, but cover the entire court when we have to make a return.

3. Competitive Rallying Drills

Competitive rallying drills pitted us against one another in a singles or doubles format with the goal of having a set of winning singles players or doubles teams. The winning player or team would then move to the next court to the right (facing the clubhouse) and the losing player or team would move to the next court to the left.

Singles

The singles competitive rally format is played on half of a court including the tramlines. Thus, there would be six or seven simultaneous competitions proceeding on three or four full courts depending on whether there were twelve or fourteen players. Each game begins with one person making a returnable underhand serve and then the two players would competitively play out the point on their half of the court. The winner of the point would make the next serve. The first player to win seven points would be the winner and would call out this fact to Tim. At that point all of the games would stop and the players who were leading would move to the right. If they were tied they would play a single point to determine the winner.

Doubles

The doubles variant of this exercise is played on a full court with two players on each side. Thus, there would be three or four games proceeding simultaneously. Like the singles it would begin with a returnable underhand serve after which the teams would play out the point. The team that won the point would make the next serve. Again, the team that was first to win seven points would call out to Tim and all winning teams would move to the right and losing teams to the left.

Sometimes, the format would be for the teams to stay together in the entire doubles session. So, you might play 30 to 40 minutes with the same partner during the doubles drill. A twist on this format would be to have us change partners each time when we moved to a new court. So, there would be shuffling up between winning and losing pairs and an opportunity to get to play with a number of different partners.

Doubles Waves

The doubles waves format seems to have been designed to give the players more of an opportunity to play at the net and thus practice their volleying technique. In this exercise both members of each doubles team would begin at the baseline. One team hits a returnable underhand serve and they play out the point. The team that wins the point would then move up to the service line and begin the next point from there with a returnable underhand serve to their opponents, who would still be at the baseline. If the team at the service line wins the point they would then move up to the net and make a returnable underhand serve from that position. If the team at the service line had lost the point they would move back to their baseline and the other team would move to their service line. A game is won when one of the teams wins the point after they have served from the net (having made two advances to get there). The teams then begin the next game at the baseline with the winners of the first game making the returnable underhand serve and the game continues until it is won by a team at the net. The first team to win seven games wins the match, with the winners moving to the court on the right and the losers to the court on the left and with the teams being broken up or kept together depending on the format being used that day.

Waves is particularly good in giving players

practice with their volleying returns since when you reach the position near the net and make a returnable underhand serve you are quite likely to have the ball bammed back at you or between you and your partner, with an occasional loop over your heads added in.

Singles/doubles combination

The singles/doubles combination is an exercise that we occasionally do in the Over-45s group. It is a bit confusing and not one of my favourites. The exercise is played on a full court with two teams of doubles players, and with three or four games proceeding simultaneously on the other courts. The exercise begins with the members of each team playing a singles game crosscourt (across the diagonal of the court: deuce half to deuce half and advantage half to advantage half). Each singles game begins with a returnable underhand serve and then both singles games proceed simultaneously cross court until one of the players wins their game at which time they call out 'doubles' and the second singles game, that is still being played, is then finished as a doubles game on the full court. A team receives a point for a singles victory and a point for a doubles victory, so the score could be 2-0 or 1-1. The subsequent games are played until one team has amassed seven points. The leading teams then move to the right and the losing teams to the left and the teams either keep the same partners on the next court or change partners as the case may be on that day.

This is a good exercise that forces you to hit the ball cross court either forehand or backhand, but is just a bit too confusing as it is frequently difficult to tell exactly when a singles game has ended and when the doubles game should begin.

Doubles champions

This is played with the doubles teams staying together for the duration of the exercise. To begin, three doubles teams are arbitrarily chosen to be the champions and they each take the north side of three doubles courts. Each one of these three champion teams is then challenged by one of the remaining three or four teams. The match begins with a returnable underhand serve from the champions after which the two teams play out the point. The challengers have to win two consecutive points after which they replace the champions. If the challengers lose either of the points they lose and they then move to any of the other courts and await a chance to play the champions of that court. This is not one of my favourite exercises as the challengers are vanquished as soon as they lose one point, while the champions must lose two consecutive points. It makes for some very rapid matches and a lot of moving around and standing waiting for a shot at one of the three champions. But, if you do become champion you have that same advantage. However, the very brief duration of each match and the constant changing of sides and courts makes this one of the less useful exercises as far as I am concerned.

Regular doubles with overhand serving tournament

We occasionally also play regular doubles with overhead serving in a tournament format in the Over-45s group, but this format is usually reserved for the last session of each term. We also sometimes play doubles with overhead serve during our weekly sessions in a similar format to the doubles with underhand serve. As I recall, the tournament format at the end of term works in the following manner. Tim picks the six teams and each match runs for ten minutes. At the end of the ten minutes Tim records the total number of points won by each team and the team with the greater number of points moves to the right and the team with the fewer points moves to the left. The process is repeated for three additional ten-minute sessions. After these four ten-minute sessions the team with the most points is crowned the tournament champion!

The Over-45s is fun. It has given me an opportunity to play tennis regularly with a group of people who are generally more experienced tennis players than I am. It also has provided a structured setting with some useful drills and, more importantly, mini competitive situations that have given me the opportunity to become familiar with actual competitions with winners and losers. And it gave me the opportunity to meet a very nice group of people and to have an enjoyable morning with them each week. After I had attended the Over-45s for a few months I was considered to be a regular member of that group. It was through the Over-45s that I met several people, mainly Mike and Sam, with whom I began to play competitive singles friendlies on a regular basis, usually for two or three sets. By the end of the second year of tennis I was playing at least twice weekly and often three or four times a week. Tennis was fast becoming an important focus in my life!

CHAPTER FOUR

Singles Friendlies

A really big challenge for me in my attempt to improve my tennis game was to find people who would be willing to play singles friendlies with me. My only pool of potential players was from the Over-45s group that I played with on Monday mornings. I was the most, or one of the most, inexperienced players in that group, so it was difficult to approach the better players about getting together on our own. And, the Over-45s was a rather chummy group of people who knew one another fairly well, so it wasn't easy to break into their circle as a novice player. Not being able to break into the Over-45s group I eventually started to play occasional singles friendlies with people whom I had met around the club and who I really didn't know.

I was soon to find out that many tennis players are highly competitive and that winning, as opposed to enjoying a relaxed game, was the primary goal of the endeavour. Being a complete novice at the game, I was not consumed by a compelling need to win. On the contrary, I am a very non-competitive person and one of the psychological barriers that I had to contend with was this rather uncompetitive nature. It wasn't that I didn't try hard; I tried very hard and enjoyed winning. I would even go over matches while I lay in bed at night trying to fall asleep, or even after awakening during the middle of the night to use the loo, as one does in one's 70s. There were times when I even had trouble falling asleep at night as I saw tennis balls coming at me from all directions, much as one might have trouble falling asleep after having driven a car at night on a road with glaring lights continually approaching.

It was not that I did not want to play well and win. But, early on I noticed that I let up a bit if my opponent became anxious if I had won a series of games, and especially if they would begin to challenge my calls as to whether their serve was in or whether their return was out on my side of the court. I found that I tended to favour my opponent with these close calls, and particularly with my calls at my baseline and after a long rally. I wouldn't just give my opponent a point out of stupid generosity and just to make them happy, but on very close calls I almost always favoured my opponent, especially when I was uncertain of the call.

I should say that making calls was one of the things that I liked least about tennis and I frequently wished that I would have an impartial umpire to release me from this burden. Calling serves in or out was not too difficult as the call is right in front of you and because part of the mental preparation to return a serve is the preparation to determine whether or not it is actually in the service box. However, when an opponent would hit a hard (good) serve that might have been just beyond the service line I would tend to give him the advantage on the call and would play the ball, since it is difficult to see whether or not it caught the line when the ball is between your line of vision and the service line. I would feel uncharitable if I deprived someone of a good serve, whereas I would be much more likely to call a fault on a weak serve in the same position. Calls on the side lines of the service box were easier to make as you could more easily see the space between the line and a ball that is out.

I found the situation to be similar in making calls during a rally. Side line calls were easier to make as one could usually see some space between the ball and the line if the shot was out, but baseline calls were much more problematic for me as, again. when a ball is just long it is difficult to see the space when you are standing behind it. I found it particularly difficult to make calls on long balls that were right at my feet in the centre of the baseline. You don't have an angle from which you can view a return that is at your feet and which is just long, and I found that I was so busy playing these shots – whether to take it on the fly as a volley; whether to half-volley it on the short hop; or whether to move back to get a more level swing -- that I found it difficult to carefully watch the baseline and impossible to call some of them, and usually treated them as in even if I strongly suspected that they were long.

However, as my game improved a bit I eventually became friendly with Mike and with Sam from the Over-45s group, who were both very compatible, and they became the first people with whom I regularly played singles friendlies.

Mike

Mike was about 65 years of age and he had only started playing tennis about two-years before me. So he was no expert at all at that time and was still in the process of breaking into the inner circle of the

better players among the Over-45s, but he was quite
sporty and had played cricket throughout his life.
Mike was quite a bit better than I, but I was getting
good enough so that I could provide him with a
somewhat competitive match. I rarely took a set
from him, but I made him move around and
provided him with a chance to play a match that he
had no anxiety about winning, thus he could try out
some things with me and enjoy it in a relaxed and
friendly manner.

Mike and I would usually play three-sets,
although we would frequently, especially me, be a
bit tired by the third set. It was after having played
three very competitive sets against Mike on one day
that I noticed how tiring three sets of singles were
for my ageing body. I would usually be a bit stiff
after a three-set match, but I would feel relatively
ok the next day. On this particular occasion I had
scheduled a friendly on the following day with a
woman who was an occasional member of the
Over-45s. Although she had been playing all of her
life and had a rather good ground game, she had a
weak serve and even at this point in my tennis
development I was regularly able to come out ahead
against her. On this occasion, the day after my
tough three-set friendly with Mike, I remember
losing to her something like 6-1 before struggling to
a 7-5 victory in our second set. What was striking to
me was how tired I was after that previous day's
match with Mike, although I was completely
unaware of it. I was not noticeably fatigued and I
still covered the court well. And my serve was not
off much from its normal mediocre self. But, I
found that the strength, or firmness, in my legs was
gone and that they were a bit wobbly. And I noticed

that I was not setting my feet and bending for the ball, but was merely getting somewhere near it and reaching for it.

Although I had not played competitive sports for years except for a bit of squash as a graduate student in my 20s, I did not have a recollection of myself becoming tired while playing. And, I had found that I did not become obviously tired as a 70-year-old running around for two or possibly three sets of singles. However, I now found that in order to play better my 70-year-old body required some rest, at least at my current level of conditioning, after three sets of singles and that it would definitely be to my advantage to take a day off between three-set matches. This was a rather difficult realisation to accept as it was a further confirmation of the fact that I am now an older person (an OAP, or old age pensioner, in the local parlance) and not the 16-year-old who played basketball all afternoon and into the evening!

Mike had a fairly strong first serve when we first started to play, but had a bit of trouble getting it in. It was not an overpowering serve and I could usually return it fairly well. His second serve was much easier to handle. However, I soon learned that returning a strong serve was only part of the problem, and that the greater challenge was to return it so that your opponent is not given an easy shot that he/she can take advantage of. At first, I just tried to return serves directly to the middle of my opponent's court, being concerned mainly about not hitting it too long. It became obvious that keeping the ball on the court was only the first step, and that against any decent opponent it was necessary to send your return to a place that would disadvantage him.

Since most people, particularly at my level or somewhat above, have better forehands than backhands, it became clear that my goal in returning a serve should be to try to get it to my opponent's backhand with as much pace as possible. Given my level of inexpertise, the above was easier said than done, yet it took me quite a while to see the importance of placement as opposed to merely returning the ball. I also eventually learned that it is additionally desirable to get your return as deep as possible in the court so that your opponent would not have the advantage of taking your return half-way up the court at the service line, or further, a position from which you will have less time to react to his shots and from which he will likely have very good angles. I also quickly, or eventually, learned that a short return also gave your opponent the opportunity to just drop it over the net as you had to stay back in anticipation of his aggressive return somewhere deep in your court.

Therefore, I tried to keep it deep and to Mike's backhand with some success. But, again, it is easier said than done. I could aim deep and to the backhand, but at my level of expertise the ball did not necessarily go there. And when you hit deep and to your opponent's backhand you run the risk of hitting the ball either too long or wide. That was a recurring problem early on as I tried to aggressively go deep and hard and to the backhand corner. It eventually dawned on me that keeping the ball on the court came first and positioning came afterwards.

Thinking about where to place my returns was one thing, but actually returning them was another.

Mike is a decent player and he was not just hitting his returns midway down the centre of the court. He was doing to me what I was trying to do to him, hitting deep to my backhand as much as possible. And, he kept me deep in the court, behind the baseline, by spraying his shots deep to my backhand and deep to my forehand. Mike also was particularly good at dropping his returns short, just over the net, and usually to the backhand side of my court. That was a good strategy against me as I was, and still am, not particularly good at volleying (hitting the ball on the fly before it bounces) and consequently tend to play deep in the court and almost never move in to volley after my serve.

My serve is not strong enough to keep a strong opponent like Mike behind the baseline, so he could make his returns well forward and keep me deep in my court. He was also quite successful with drop shots on my second serves. From playing with Mike, and with some other people that I subsequently played with as well, I learned that drop shots, just over the net and especially to the backhand side of your opponent's court, could be extremely effective if executed properly. That is if they stay flat and don't loop up too high so that your opponent will have time to come in on it. And, they are also effective if your opponent is deep in his court and not moving forward.

Against me Mike played a rather aggressive game of serve and volley. Thus, if he got a good first serve in he often would come toward the net in an attempt to hit my return on the fly (before it bounces) and to hit it back hard and at a sharp angle toward the side lines. Mike was very good at volleying and it was an effective strategy against me off of a strong first serve, particularly to my backhand. Being fairly tall, about 6' 3" or so, and with long arms, I found Mike to be a bit intimidating as he charged toward the net. And seeing forward movement like that in your visual field compels you to take your eye off the approaching ball a bit and forces you to make a decision as to how you are going to respond.

Initially, my response to Mike coming to the net on his serve or during a rally was to try to lob my return over his head deep in his court. That was sometimes successful, particularly if I had an easy return, but I found that too often I tended to lob my return long, beyond the baseline, and would lose the point, or I would not lob it long enough and he would be able to slam it back at me, or that my lob would be long enough and would stay in his court but that he would be able to recover and return it. Furthermore, I found that the time taken in the thought process involved in deciding whether to lob or hit a regular return often led to a muffled lob or a weak return.

My solution to the lob dilemma when my opponent comes forward to the net is to avoid making the lob and to make the return as hard as I can and to his backhand side. Knowing what I am going to do beforehand has allowed me to avoid the decision time problem, and staying away from the lob has helped me side step the calibration necessary to determine the height and the depth of the lob so that I avoid the slam return and yet manage to keep the ball on the court. I'm not sure that my solution is best for everyone, and there are occasions when I still use a lob, but a forceful return well to the backhand of a forward moving opponent has become my standard defence against an opponent coming to the net, unless if I am deep in my own court when I might then try to loop (not lob) my return long to my opponents backhand side.

Mike played more frequently than I and had weekly coaching lessons and eventually became a much better player than myself. But, I always enjoyed playing with him and feel that I learned much of what I know about tennis by playing with Mike and watching him play.

Sam

Sam was the other person with whom I played singles friendlies on a regular basis during the first two-years of my tennis career. He was about 53-years old and had recently retired. Sam had played tennis throughout his life, but had not played regularly in recent years and although he was better than I his game was quite rusty. His serve was stronger than mine, but quite erratic and he double faulted with some frequency, which was to my advantage in a match. However, he soon learned to ease up on his second serve to make sure that it got it in the service box as it became apparent to him that my returns were not that punishing and that it was a better bet for him to give me a swing at a weak second serve than run the high risk that his brisk second serve would be out.

Our matches tended to be fairly even with each of us usually winning one of the two sets we played, and since they were more even than my matches with Mike they ran longer so we rarely played a third set. It was nice to play with someone I had a chance of beating, as that was not the case with

Mike. Yet, at this relatively early stage of my tennis-playing career I was somewhat uncomfortable when I beat my opponent as I felt that they were angry in some way for having lost to an obvious novice like me, and felt more at ease if I had played a close match which I had actually lost. Winning or losing did not matter too much to me at this point and I felt better about calling my opponent's close, but obviously out, shot as out if they were leading, but would more likely call it in if I were ahead. Later on as the game became more natural to me I became much more at ease with calls one way or another.

It was fun to play with Sam. He covered the court very well and frequently surprised me by returning shots that I thought were beyond his reach. He was particularly good at returning my deep shots to his backhand corner and I have vivid pictures of him in my mind racing across the court and somehow getting his wristed extended at an angle that allowed him to hit my well-placed hopeful winner back to my side of the court. In contrast, I had great difficulty getting behind a looping, high-bouncing return to my backhand as I just was not able in the course of play to extend my wrist far enough to pull my return onto the court as opposed to slicing it beyond the side line.

Like me, Sam did not come to the net much and was not great at volleying, although he was better than I was. Our matches tended to be played at the baseline with a few drop shots mixed in. I think that it was while playing with Sam that I learned that drop shots were much more effective when you were hitting them into the wind than when the wind was coming from behind. On some days the wind was a significant factor, and it was necessary to be well aware of its direction. A drop shot hit into the wind had a much better chance of being held up and of dying short on the court, while a drop shot hit with the wind behind you tended to carry and bounce higher and be less effective.

There was one occasion in an early match with Sam when I remember being murdered by his drop shots and it was only after a while that I figured out that they were almost always coming when he was hitting into the wind. I soon learned to move up a bit when I had the wind at my back to guard against the drop shot, which I could do since he was hitting into the wind and it would be more difficult for him to drive his deep shots past me. And, I learned to use the drop shot myself, mostly when I was hitting into the wind, and I learned that when one has the wind at your back you will have more velocity on your returns and that is the time to try to drive your shots past your opponent.

I also learned that I had to carefully calibrate my deep returns with respect to whether I was hitting into or with the wind. With a moderate to strong wind coming at you, you really have to hit the ball hard to get any pace on it and to keep it deep in your opponent's court. In contrast, when the wind is at your back you can get good velocity on your returns if you hit them hard, but you have to make sure that you keep the ball low or it will likely carry too far. However, being aware of the effects of the wind is one thing and effectively adjusting your game to the wind conditions on a particular day is another, and I frequently had the problem of sending my returns too long, beyond the baseline, when I was hitting with the wind coming from behind.

Because we were evenly matched Sam became my main partner for singles friendlies. And, we were really beginning to become friends as well. It was thus quite a disappointment to me when Sam announced that he and his wife were moving. It had been extremely difficult to find someone at or slightly above my level of tennis expertise who was available to play once or twice weekly. Sam fit that bill and he was a nice guy. And he enjoyed playing with me. He was not one of the better men players among the Over-45s who would occasionally play a friendly with me because I had asked, but who felt that I was really below their level.

Other Singles Partners

I still have not really recovered, tennis-wise, from the loss of Sam as a partner for singles friendlies. There are several chaps with whom I play on occasion, but have not found anyone who is about at my level and who is available and willing to play regularly. It was also a significant personal loss as I was becoming friendly with Sam and was hoping that our friendship would extend beyond tennis. One of the pleasures of tennis for me is that it has put me into contact with a whole new group of people and I was hoping that contact would lead to some new friendships for me personally, friendships outside those I already have here with and through my wife and outside those from my academic connections.

From early on I did play singles friendlies with a number of women whom I knew first from my Beginner's Course and later from the Over-45s. The one woman that I played with from the Beginner's Course was the first person with whom I ventured out onto the club courts outside of the security of that group coaching session, but her playing was at too low a level for it to be much fun or much of a challenge for me, so that did not go too far. However, I did play a bit with several women from the Over-45s. One was probably in her mid-50s and had been playing all of her life, but had just started to play more regularly. She had a good ground game and a mediocre serve, and at that stage of my career I had to play hard in order to beat her. What struck me though was that winning seemed so important to her and winning or losing became a somewhat constant topic of conversation during our matches. Losing 6-2, 6-3, 6-4 or whatever doesn't bother me as long as I have played as well as I could and had an enjoyable time. With this friend I found that I had to ease up on my game on many occasions in order to keep the score comfortable for her. That wasn't much fun as she was really a fairly good tennis player who would have been much more competitive if she could have improved her serve a bit. I also played occasional singles with another woman from the Over-45s group, but that petered out as well. Although she had great form and would occasionally play very well in a doubles format in the Over-45s, she didn't hold up very well against me in singles and seemed to mind the fact that she was not winning.

Alice is now the only woman with whom I play singles friendlies with any frequency. She is in her early 50s and is quite sporty, but has only been playing tennis a year or two longer than I. She regularly attends the Over-45s and is a central person in that group. She is a very, very pleasant and welcoming person and although I feel that we are only acquaintances she is a person whom I like very much. Alice takes her tennis quite seriously and has been taking once-weekly lessons from Tim for several years. She seems to live on the tennis courts, always playing singles and doubles friendlies as well as her mini-league singles matches. Alice is a tall woman who hits the ball hard and plays an aggressive game with a very strong backhand.

More than a year ago I played Alice several times and beat her in close matches. This past year we have split the few matches we have played. But, she now plays much more than me and has had consistent coaching and I suspect that she will now beat me on a regular basis. I am writing this in August 2014, toward the end of the summer, and have been away from tennis for five weeks due to holiday travel and for several weeks due to a toe injury. I'm thinking about who my tennis friendly partners will be for the coming year and hope that I will be able to arrange regular 'hits' with Alice. My stock among the Over-45s will go down if she beats me regularly, but that really doesn't matter to me as I prefer to play against someone who is slightly better than I and losing to a woman, at my current age or at any age, is no big deal for me. There are several chaps who I also have in mind for singles friendlies, but they are all better than I and are less available during the day. And, I am hoping that Mike will continue to be interested in an occasional 'hit' with me although I fear that he may have found better players than me for friendlies.

CHAPTER FIVE

Lessons With Tim

Mike, Alice, and several of my other tennis mates had been taking individual lessons and I decided to do so as well. One obviously gets a certain amount of practice hitting the ball in a friendly, but our rallies (hitting the ball back and forth while playing for a point) tend to be relatively short and we spend a fair amount of time serving and picking up the balls between points. And, there tends to be a fair amount of group instruction during the 12 to 14 person Over-45s group. Individual one-hour lessons with one of the coaches involves almost continuous hitting with occasional instruction as you go, so it is an ideal way to get more practice with your strokes.

Mike was taking lessons from one of the women coaches and Alice took her lessons with Tim, who is about 32-years-old and who ran the Over-45s group. From speaking with Mike it seemed that they worked a lot on correct technique, while Tim seemed to focus a tiny bit less on perfect technique and correct form with the older players and more on getting in as many hits as possible. Tim is quite jovial and non-judgemental while the female coaches seemed to be more reserved. I aspire to have good technique and to develop good form, but was finding that despite being told what was correct my 70-year-old mind and body found it difficult to completely put that instruction into practice. My forehand and backhand grips just seemed to be what they were and not what they should be and my chopper volleying grip just seemed to slide into my forehand grip. I felt that I needed greater attention to technique to help me deal with these problems, but I didn't want to be held up with too much instruction and not get enough practice hitting the ball. So, I made arrangements with Tim for a one-hour session each week for three months in order to see whether that would work for me.

As hoped for, Tim did not relentlessly concentrate on correct technique and more or less allowed me to have a go at it while making many useful suggestions along the way. At this point in my development I felt that I just needed the opportunity to get as much practice as I could so that I could find a swing that was comfortable for me and, more importantly, a forehand and backhand swing that was reasonably effective.

The Club has many junior programmes for children from about the age of five on up, and I frequently saw these junior players either in group lessons or playing among themselves or having individual lessons with the coaches. To me it was amazing how well some of these juniors played, particularly once they reached about ten-years-of-age. By age 12 some of these kids were absolutely terrific. What was most striking was that their technique was perfect, that is, they were doing all of the things that I had been told to do and had so much trouble doing, and they were doing it perfectly – like little Roger Federers or diminutive Maria Sharapovas! And, I felt embarrassed to play on an adjacent or nearby court in the presence of these little prodigies!

It was a situation similar to that which one encounters with the acquisition of a foreign language. I never had the opportunity to live in a foreign country as a youth and thus acquire the ability to speak a foreign language by immersion in that culture at an early age. I did learn some Spanish and French in secondary school and eventually became a reasonably fluent Spanish speaker when I spent over a year in Ecuador doing my doctoral research when I was in my 30s. But, I do not speak absolutely fluently and as naturally as I would have had I been immersed in a Spanish-speaking milieu at five or six or seven-years-of-age.

Now, since my retirement and since my relocation to England when I was in my 60s, I have been trying to improve my ability to speak French as my wife and I have several friends who have vacation houses there and we find that we are frequently travelling to that lovely country. However, although I have been studying and practicing French on and off over the past eight years, I only speak in a serviceable manner and not with great fluency. In contrast my wife Jenny, who spent a month annually in southwest France with the family of her friend Nicole during her teenage years, speaks with a fluency that I am sure that I will never attain at this point of my life. And, I doubt that Jenny would achieve much fluency in Spanish if she would take it up now that she is in her 70s!

So it is with tennis! I am afraid that I am a victim of my years. Irrespective of how much I try and how much I practice, I will never have the tennis form and fluency of those youngsters who have been playing regularly since they were six or seven-years-old. And, it is unlikely that I will ever have the form and be as good a player as my contemporaries who have been playing since their youths and throughout much of their lives.

It was with great determination, but not great expectations, that I ploughed ahead with my lessons with Tim. As I said, it was mostly hitting sessions with useful instruction, and that is what I wanted. At first it was mainly to my forehand and I would return anywhere on his court. Then it was to my forehand and I was to return it alternatively to his forehand and then to his backhand. And then it was to my backhand in the same manner – any return, cross-court returns, and down-the-line returns. Tim kept up a fairly rapid pace and I soon found that these sessions were quite tiring. I was getting what I wanted, more hitting in a single one-hour session than I was probably getting in a month of my once-a-week Over-45s sessions and twice-weekly friendlies! I needed this kind of practice and I wondered whether I could get it by just 'hitting' like this with some of my Over-45s mates, but everyone wanted to play competitive games and not just hit the ball back and forth – probably because most of them have been playing tennis so long that rallying back and forth is not what they think of as tennis.

I continued my sessions with Tim over the weeks and it was clear that they were helping me. My forehand was becoming stronger and my rather weak backhand was improving and I was beginning to have more pace and better placement on my returns. After a while I told Tim that in my competitive games one of the many weaknesses that I felt that I had was moving in to make a backhand return near the service line. I was having trouble setting my feet and bending properly and seemed to be stretching rather than bending and was hitting the ball on the run without much control.

I vividly remember one session we had in which we worked on this issue. I stood at the baseline and Tim would hit the ball softly over the net to my backhand side and I would run in to make the return. I would then rapidly retreat back to the baseline and the process would be repeated. Therefore, I was constantly on the move running in to make sometimes awkward backhand returns and then racing back to the baseline for the next go – a rather exhausting exercise. At one point Tim chuckled and said that I looked like an elephant lumbering in to make my returns and that I should try to 'float in like Roger Federer'. Being a 72-year-old man who had spinal surgery on his back two years previously, I didn't think that it was likely that I would ever be able to emulate Roger Federer, or even anyone in the top 500,000!

My lessons continued for about three months, the period we had agreed upon, at which time we were going away for holiday for two or three weeks, and I thought that this might be a good point at which to stop my coaching sessions with Tim. I found that my 72-year-old body was too tired to play a competitive game after my coaching sessions on Wednesdays and that I rarely had a chance to play singles after the one-and-a-half hour session of the Over-45s on Mondays. Therefore, there were only three other days during the week – Tuesdays, Thursdays, and Fridays -- in which to fit my singles matches as I didn't like to play on weekends when it was very busy and difficult to get a court and when much of the court time was devoted to social doubles.

However, the primary reason that I decided to end my coaching sessions with Tim was because I was reaching the point in the development of my game at which I was realising that there is more to tennis than returning the ball with some pace, but that there is strategy involved in the game and that the best way to develop a sense of that strategy and a sense of how you perform in a game is to play as many games as possible against a variety of opponents. And, I was beginning to sense that while my singles friendlies were quite enjoyable and often quite competitive, it might also be a good idea to enter into a truly competitive situation. I therefore asked Tim about the club mini-league competition and asked him to recommend my placement in one of the divisions.

CHAPTER SIX
The Mini-League

The Club singles mini-league is a competitive ladder that players ascend or descend as they win or lose their matches. Looking at the roster for Round 4 of the Summer 2014 session, it is made up of 31 Divisions with each division having five players, both men and women. Each player in a division plays a match against each other player in their division. Thus, you have four matches to play and this must be accomplished over a period of about four weeks. The roughly 160 participants in the mini-league represent about 35 percent of the approximately 450 senior members of the club. Mini-league participants are not necessarily the best players in the club, although at the top divisions they usually are, but merely those who have the time and the inclination to deal with the logistical demands of this activity. The Winter sessions have seven players in each division and fewer divisions and run for about seven weeks.

I am currently in the 27th division, thus placing me roughly in the lower quarter of the table. Among my mates from the Over-45s group Mike is in Division 19, Paul is in the 20th division, and George is in the 24th division. My buddy Alice is currently in the 29th division, but she usually is just one division below me. Alan, who occasionally plays in the Over-45s, is usually around the 15th division, but I don't see his name on this summer's list.

Several of the better men players in the Over-45s group do not play in the mini-league and at the moment Alice is the only woman from that group who is participating. The logistics of arranging matches can be quite a hassle and some people do not want to have to add another organisational problem to their lives. Other people, I suppose, enjoy playing friendlies rather than finding themselves ranked on a competitive ladder. Also, I suspect that some of the chaps don't relish the prospect of losing to the female players in the mini league, many of whom are quite good.

I started in the mini-league after I had been playing for about a year-and-a-half and my position was probably about the same as now, in the lower quarter of the ladder. The division number that you are in really does not mean that much as the number of divisions changes from season to season and year to year as members choose whether or not to play and people leave the club and new members join. However, by looking at the names of the players I can see that I am about a division or two lower than the group of player that I started with, all of whom are much younger than myself. Among the Over-45s, Mike has moved up quite a bit and Paul has moved up as well compared to me.

One thing that I noticed immediately in the mini-league is that people are much more competitive and that some players are likely to challenge me when I call one of their returns on my side of the court out. And, I had the strong impression that an occasional opponent is not scrupulously honest when they called some of my returns on their side of the court long. However, that was a relatively minor issue, but I did find that I could not be entirely passive about things and that it was probably useful to speak up and good-naturedly question what I thought were dubious calls.

Another thing that I found which reflected the competitive nature of the mini-league matches is that certain opponents on very rare occasions appeared to misrepresent the score. In friendlies we would occasionally, or even frequently, be uncertain of the score of a game, but we would always resolve the uncertainty amiably, particularly since we were friends who regularly played together. And, being in my 70s and having to think about so many different aspects of the game that was still new to me, I found that it was not infrequent that I would lose track of the score. But, playing in a competitive situation against some players who you do not know, or hardly know, one loses track of the score at one's peril. I found that it was necessary to really concentrate on keeping track of the score and to repeat the score out loud after each point, and that it seemed that on very rare occasions one of my opponents would alter the score to their advantage if I naively asked what the score was. On one occasion I remember having lost a match 7-4, but after we gathered our things together my opponent said that the score had been 8-3 as she trotted off to post the results on the mini-league score sheet in the club house – an unlikely error. To deal with this problem, one of my mini-league opponents kept a pile of stones on the side of the court with the number of our respective games won in each pile, but I was a bit dubious of this manoeuver as it was hard to see the piles from the other side of the court as the stones were added after each game so I made especially sure that I called out the score of the match after each game as well.

A mini-league match at the Club is made up of eleven games. The first ten are regular games and the eleventh is played as a tie-break. The scores, in terms of games won for each player in a match, are then posted on the mini-league chart in the clubhouse. Thus, each player in a division would accumulate a number of games won over the course of the four week session. If there are five players in a division the maximum games won that you can accumulate in a session would be 44 (four 11-0 wins) and the minimum number of games won that you could have would be zero (four 0-11 losses). At the end of the session the one or two players in each division who had the most wins would move up to the next highest division and the one or two players with the fewest wins would move down to the next lowest division. That is generally the way that it works with some additional adjustment that is beyond my current knowledge.

Thus, in general, with each new session the membership of each division would change with one or two players dropping down into it from the next highest division and one or two players moving up into it from the next lowest division. However, things did not work out exactly like that as new players would join the mini-league continually and people participating in it would drop out of a session because they would be away on holiday or business or because they just wanted a break from competitive tennis.

People in the Over-45s were quite aware of how someone from that group was doing in the mini-league. I remember vividly the acclaim accorded to me by one of the female members of the Over-45s after I had beaten a very formidable female member of the Over-45s in the mini-league. The person according me this acclaim did not play in the mini-league herself, and I had not mentioned this victory to her, but she seemed to know about it from the Over-45s grapevine. I should mention that my formidable opponent must have had an off-day when she played me on that occasion as she subsequently thrashed me quite badly when we played again at a later date.

The mini-league has been very good for me in that I have had the opportunity to play against a number of different opponents in a fairly competitive setting. At first I was quite tense about playing in a situation where the score of my match would become a publically recorded event and with the possibility that I would be repeatedly beaten quite badly. But, I got used to the situation and Tim had placed me at approximately the correct level so that my early experiences were a mixture of successes and failures.

I don't think that the pressure of a competitive match bothered me that much. When I played Mike I would invariably lose, thus I would play hard, but with little expectation of winning a set, although I did do so on rare occasions. And with Sam it was not much of a concern. We were rather evenly matched and it didn't matter who won or lost as our scores in each set were usually quite close. However, I really wanted to win my mini-league matches, although, of course, it was not the most important thing in the world. I usually started out playing fairly aggressively (for me) and on many occasions would find that I had a bit of a lead, say 3-1 or 4-2. It would be at that point that I would feel the pressure to win and would begin to play more conservatively, not going for the corners as much and not trying to place my returns at the baseline in order to avoid hitting it too long.

I found that growing conservatism when I had a lead to be my main negative response to pressure. My response to the pressure of being behind in a match has probably been a tendency to get a bit desperate and try too hard to put the ball deep and in my opponent's backhand corner and to neglect his forehand corner and the occasional drop shot. I also noticed that when I fall rather far behind my service game become a bit automatic. I don't breathe deeply before serving and I tend to serve right down the middle without attempting much placement of my serves.

I also have noticed how pressure affects my opponents. In some matches I have sensed that my winning the first game of the match was a bit intimidating to my opponent, and on other occasions I have noticed that my opponents gain confidence and play more aggressively and better after they have won a few consecutive games against me.

When I win the flip of the racket I have frequently struggled to decide whether to choose to serve or to receive. A good player with a good serve will usually choose to serve as the likelihood of someone with a good serve winning his service game is high and it is a nice advantage to be ahead and for your opponent to be under pressure to have to win his service game. However, I have an adequate but mediocre serve and have frequently wondered whether it is advantageous for me to serve first and run the risk of losing the game or to chance allowing my opponent to serve first with the hope that I could break his serve and gain a psychological advantage. However, I suspect that most of my opponents would think that I am wacky if I allowed them to serve first, so I usually bow to that imagined pressure and take the first serve if I can. Nevertheless, if we are in a bit of a rush to get started due to a court scheduling issue or the threat of rain and I am not adequately warmed up, then I will frequently allow my opponent to serve first with the hope that my shoulder and legs will be more limber when it comes my time to serve.

When playing in the mini-league I became further aware of the necessity of knowing the direction and force of the wind. Some of the women in their 40s and 50s who I have played against are not especially heavy hitters, but they have been playing tennis for many years and are rather savvy opponents. They are very steady in a rally and move the ball well from side to side. And, if they are hitting the ball into the wind they tend to be quite clever in employing a drop shot more than occasionally. At first, I couldn't understand why I was being caught flatfooted by these soft returns until I realised that they were being hit into the wind and that I was not compensating for that fact by playing in a bit in front of the baseline.

Another thing I began to notice in the mini-league was that several of my opponents, seemed to try to speed up the pace of the match, especially if I was winning. Most of my opponents in the mini-league are quite a bit younger than I am – usually in their in their 30s, 40s or 50s and maybe one or two in their early 60s. There are good players who are in their 60s, but they must be scattered through the higher (lower numbered) divisions. My sense is that some of my female opponents who are experienced, but not outstanding, tennis players are the ones who seem to employ this speed-up tactic against me.

I play a very active game of tennis and move around the court as well as most people over 50. But, at 72-years-of-age I do become a bit tired after a long rally that required constant movement from one side of the court to another. In those circumstances, particularly if I am serving, I will tend to pick up a ball from the court and put it in my pocket as a way of having an extra 15 seconds or so to catch my breath. Or, if my opponent is serving I might take out my handkerchief to blow my nose – which I do with some frequency throughout the match as I tend to have a slightly runny nose.

What I have noticed is that some of my opponents, who are usually much younger than me, will be preparing to serve before I have even moved into position to receive their serve. My defence against these hurry-up tactics is to face away from them completely and then turn quickly and be ready to receive their serve. I understand that matches should be played at a reasonable pace, but I do play my matches at a reasonable pace and we are not in a tournament and are only playing 11 games in a full mini-league match and we also have to gather up our own balls. So, from my point of view there is no need for them to unduly speed up the pace of the match, especially since they know that they are playing against someone who is obviously in his 70s!

After having played in the mini-league for a while I began to become aware of the issue of fitness and the related issue of my age. I noticed that I would frequently have a substantial lead in a match – 3-1, or 4-2 or 5-3 – and then find that my opponent would come roaring back to either leave me with either a close victory or a defeat. At first I imputed it to the fact that, as noted previously, I tend to play more conservatively when I am in the lead and lose my aggressive attacking edge. However, I also began to entertain the fact that it was possible that I was fatiguing a bit as the match progresses and it was for that reason that I was losing my edge.

The mini-league matches are only 11 games, so I doubt that that in itself is a fatiguing experience for me. When I played friendlies with Mike or with Sam I would play at least two and sometimes three sets and would not be noticeably tired in the second set, although fatigue would be more apparent in the third set. And, I had noticed that if I played again the day after I had played three-sets my game was quite visibly off.

What I began to see was that playing tennis three or four times a week was ok if I was playing friendlies when winning or losing is not that important, but that I must have a day or even two days off before a mini-league match to allow my 72-year-old body to recover and to thus maximise my chance of winning. Without the two-days rest I can still get on the court and run around and play fairly well, but I think that what happens is that I tire just a bit and don't bend my knees when I am hitting the ball but just reach for the ball instead. I also have noticed that as I tire my serve becomes more automatic and less planned in that I tend not to think much about placement.

So, I have attempted to be more judicious in

scheduling my mini-league matches and try to arrange them so that I have at least one, and preferably two, days' rest between two or three-set singles friendlies and mini-league matches, and even between mini-league matches themselves. Saying that makes me feel like a bit of a wimp as I see some of my 30 and 40-year-old mini-league opponents playing multiple mini-league matches on the same day on weekends. However, two 11-game mini-league matches one after the other is only slightly more tennis playing than two competitive sets of tennis, and these people who play on weekends are probably not retired and work during the week and thus probably have had five days rest between their two consecutive weekend mini-league matches! Irrespective, in order to improve my fitness I have recently joined a gym in a senior living complex with which my wife has an association and have started, with the help of an excellent trainer, doing a programme of exercises to strengthen my legs. I go there for a weekly session with the trainer and occasionally on my own to work out while the 80 and 90-year-olds are getting help with their balance.

CHAPTER SEVEN

Playing Tennis Outdoors In Winter

The tennis club where I play only has outdoor courts. There are no bubbles or indoor courts. Currently, there are thirteen surfaced courts and two grass courts. There are seven carpet surface type courts, three hard-surface courts, three courts that are called 'clay courts' but which really have a carpet surface with sand or clay or some other grainy material on them, and two grass courts.

Most people try to play their matches on the carpet-surfaced courts while the hard surface courts tend to be used more for juniors programs and some group lessons. The 'clay' courts are also nice to play on, but the line markings tend to fade a bit and the ball does not come up very well on this surface unless you are using new balls. The grass courts usually cannot be used before 10 am during the warmer months and are not much use when it rains or during the winter, although some people enjoy playing on them. The seven carpet courts all have lighting and can be used during the evenings.

There are certain constraints on playing given the fact that the courts are all outdoors, Rain is a constant fact of life in England and there are long periods at all times of the year when it rains often enough during the day to make playing tennis a bit of a challenge. All of the courts except the 'clay courts' can be quite slippery when wet and I, and others, have occasionally taken a slide on a wet surface, particularly early in the morning on a cold day. Snow, also, is an occasional impediment, but snow is infrequent where I live and usually occurs when cold is a greater constraint to play.

Wind is another problem, but one learns to adapt. The courts are aligned north/south and the wind is usually blowing from one of those directions or the other, although it does also frequently comes from the west. There is not a problem playing in a moderate headwind as you exchange sides after two games and just adjust your play accordingly. A strong crosswind is less common and is much more difficult to play in as the ball can take unusual bends and returns near the side line where the wind is exiting the court can easily be blown out, while if you are aiming for the side line where the wind is entering the court you actually have to hit it down the tramlines with the hope that it will be blown back onto the singles court. These difficulties tend to encourage a game played in the middle of the court. The one or two mini-league matches that I had scheduled and which we decided to cancel when we arrived on court were both when there were very strong crosswinds, which is tolerable for a friendly but not ideal conditions for a more competitive match.

You can always at least try to arrange your friendlies and your mini-league matches taking the weather into consideration. If it is raining or very cold you can just telephone/text/email your opponent and call off the match. But, the Over-45s were held on Mondays at 9:30 throughout the year, and Tim ran his sessions under almost all conditions. Therefore, if you wanted the tennis practice and the social joviality of that group you had to attend no matter what the weather. This was really only a concern in winter when it could be as low as -2 C (28 F) at 9:30 am on a cold morning and between 0 to 2 C (32 -36 F) on many days, although it would warm up to 5-7 C (41-45 F) by the time the session would end at 11 am.

These chilling winter morning conditions created a culture of toughing it out among a group of eight to ten regular participants in the Over-45s group. This group of non-expert, but anxious to improve their game enthusiasts, would show up with heavy jackets and hats and gloves and complain bitterly (pardon the pun) about the cold, but would feel quite sanctimonious about being out and on the courts under in these challenging conditions. It would usually warm up somewhat by 10 to 10:30 and the winter gear would come off to varying degrees.

I don't mind the cold that much and I never used gloves. What did bother me was when the carpet courts would be slick early in the morning as a consequence of dew or precipitation and cold. I slipped at least twice under these conditions, but one learns to adjust one's playing, particularly during a practice session like the Over-45s, to the conditions and to slow down one's game accordingly.

I don't at all enjoy playing indoors. I dislike the high bounce of the ball on the hard court surfaces that I have encountered the few times that I have played indoors, and I particularly do not like the overhead lights which I find somewhat blinding not only when I serve but throughout a rally as well. And, I do not like the precisely restricted court times and the impatient players who are next-up and who are waiting on the side line. Nevertheless, if you want to play tennis in the dead of winter in England, and if you wish to play under dry conditions and without having to combat the wind, then indoor tennis – at least during the winter – may be the answer for you. But I like the trees and the birds and the fresh air and the greater availability of the outdoor courts, so I will stick to that if you please!

CHAPTER EIGHT

Doubles

Doubles is a very different kind of game than singles tennis. I have been playing doubles for less than a year now and am not particularly good at it. The amount of movement, the strategy and the returns one makes require a very different approach than singles. As you know, doubles is played with two players on each side and the court is slightly wider than the singles court, with the outer of the two lines on thc side of the doubles court being its width while the inner of the two side lines is the width of the singles court. In doubles the person serving usually serves from the far corner of his/her court, just inside the singles side line, while in singles most players usually serve from about a metre (yard) on either side of the midline. Starting from this position the person serving covers half the court and tends to stay deep in the court during much of the play and may also cover deep returns to his partner's side of his court. His partner is positioned forward on the other half of their court about midway between the service line and the net. The opposing team is positioned similarly, with the person receiving the serve playing deep and crosscourt to the person who is serving, and with his partner on the other half of their court positioned close to the net and directly in front of the person serving.

The problem posed by doubles is that there is a

person on the opposing team standing close to the net who is intent on hitting anything that comes near him into your court, usually with some speed. The task of the person returning the serve is to direct his return away from his opponent at the net and to a place where neither of his opponents will be able to return it.

The fact that there is an opponent close to the net makes this a very different game for me as I usually try to exploit the backhand of my opponent in a singles match. Since about 85 percent of players are right handed, this means hitting it straight ahead and down the side line when you are receiving on the deuce side of the court, rather than across the court. However, in doubles your opponent at the net is an impediment to accomplishing this. To do so you have to hit past him and down the side line (not easy to do) or over his head while making sure that you do not hit it too long. The easiest return is crosscourt, but that usually means that you are hitting right into the forehand of your opponent who has served or who has just returned your serve.

Volleying, coming up to the net and returning a ball just after it crosses the net and before it bounces, is the basis of doubles play, and I just am not particularly good at it. If one is playing at the net you have to be able to return anything coming directly at or near you and return it with a forceful and well-placed volley, and you have to be able to move toward the centre of the court to try to intercept your opponents' crosscourt returns. And, you have to protect your side line and also make sure that your opponents don't drive or loft a ball over your head to the uncovered deep portion of the court on your side.

I'm just not good at volleying! Maybe it is inexperience, or maybe my reflexes at 72-years-of-age are a bit slower than most people, or maybe it is how I am holding my racket, or maybe I am just not aggressive enough when I play at the net. Whatever the answer may be, I am a far weaker doubles player than I am at singles. The primary thing, I think, is just lack of experience playing doubles. Many of the people in the Over-45s play nothing but doubles; their entire tennis experience is playing doubles and they do it regularly. The Club also has almost daily sessions of 'social doubles' where you can come without pre-arrangement or a partner and get included into doubles play, while there is no such thing as 'social singles' where one can show up and be paired in a singles match. I have concentrated on singles and usually do not play later in the day and on weekends when most of the courts ae devoted to social doubles. But, we play some doubles in the Over-45s group and at times I become involved in a set or two of doubles after the Over-45s.

This has been the context of my initial experience with this form of the game. One of my biggest problems with doubles is that I do not cover the middle of the court very well. Because I am unsure of my volleying and am overly concerned that my opponent directly across from me will drive the ball down the side line and past my backhand, I tend to anchor myself in the middle of my half of the court and reach a bit to the centre but do not move aggressively to the centre and beyond as does Mike and some of the other better net players. When I am at the net I tend to permit my partner to carry the burden of rallying which puts him/her in the position of making the error of hitting it too close to the opposing net player. I'm also not very aggressive about coming to the net when I serve and that also is a disadvantage in doubles.

I think that I have to play more doubles and become more accustomed to playing at the net. I'm trying to have a doubles game plan pre-positioned in my head in preparation for playing doubles this coming autumn. I've decided that I am going to move more aggressively to the centre and beyond not worrying about my side line at all. If I get punished by doing so then I can always move back, but I want to see what it feels like, and how successful I can be, playing the centre of the court.

More important than position is, I believe, the fact that I am not comfortable holding my racket in the 'chopper' volleying grip and using this same grip to execute both forehand and backhand volley returns. I can use a chopper grip to make a forehand volley, but it just doesn't seem to work for my backhand volleys except in practice sessions. Instead, my natural tendency is to use a forehand grip for my forehand volleys and to then rotate to use a backhand grip to make my backhand volleys. However, rotating the racket has the significant disadvantage in that it takes time, and time is not what you have when you are standing five feet from the net and the ball is coming at you from relatively close range and with considerable speed!

Again, it seems it is the matter of having taken up tennis rather late in life and finding it difficult to hold my racket the correct way instead of the comfortable way. Despite having been playing tennis now for two-and-a-half years, hitting a good backhand volley under the uncertainties and pressures of a game – as opposed to when it is predictably served to me during practice – is still something that produces an uncertain result.

As a youth I played various kinds of baseball, softball and especially stickball with a pink rubber ball, almost continuously. Even now I can easily catch a tennis ball that is thrown or hit towards me at speed – with two hands and even with one hand. I'm sure that I could stand at the net during a doubles match and catch most balls that are hit toward me within twice the width of my body. It feels natural to me and I could do it without thinking about it. The neuromotor memory is there! My eyes see the ball coming and my hands just move to the proper place to catch it. I have no pre-programmed plan in my head about how to do it, it just happens. In contrast, my tennis racket still feels foreign in my hand, especially with respect to my grip for a backhand volley and in general as to how I play my volley game. Sometimes I cannot even remember to hold my racket up, and on more than one occasion had a ball hit right at me at the net only to find that my racket was pointing down to the ground!

I have found that there are so many different parts of the game of tennis on which one must simultaneously concentrate that volleying appears to have slipped between the cracks. My service and my ground game seem to have taken most of my attention because they are the essence of singles play, while the necessity of improving my volley has only become apparent as I have begun to play doubles.

CHAPTER NINE

The 'Tennis Ladies'

The opportunity to play more doubles came my way when a female member of the Over-45s asked whether I would be willing to fill in to make a doubles foursome with several of the women in that group. These ladies get together to play doubles several times a week and there was an extended period when one of them was not going to be available, so, after two-years of singles play I started to play doubles weekly on Tuesdays at 2:45 pm with what I began to call, in my head, the 'tennis ladies'. I'm not sure of their exact ages, but am rather certain that they are all in their early to mid-50s.

All of the 'tennis ladies' were more experienced players than I, although Alice had only been playing regularly a few years longer than I had. Alice played in the mini-league, as I did, and was one or two divisions below (higher number) than me, but the other ladies did not play on the competitive ladder and only played doubles friendlies, usually with other women and occasionally with one or two of the chaps from the Over-45s. I'm sure that I could hold my own in a singles match with any of them, although Alice is now probably a stronger player than I am. But, I was clearly the weakest doubles player in the group. At first, I really did not know what to do!

I enjoyed playing with the 'tennis ladies'. At

first, we chose sides arbitrarily and then changed sides after each set. Later, we tended to play two or three sets with the same partners on any given day and then change partners the following week. I was really surprised at how good this group was at playing doubles, and especially with their net play. Whereas I was hesitant at the net they seemed confident and whereas I seemed to anchor myself in the middle of my half of the court they would wander all over the court and aggressively pursue all returns. It seemed as though their reflexes must have been better than mine. They just seemed to be able to make fairly effective volley returns on most things that came their way at the net. In contrast, I would make the occasional good return, but would muff many easy volleys and was particularly ineffective at covering the centre of the court.

My doubles play improved a bit over time, but it certainly was not an ego boost to play with this group. However, they were very gracious to include me in their weekly sessions and it seemed to me to be a good way to get started playing doubles by playing with people that I know and playing on a regular basis. The chaps from the Over-45s –Mike, Paul, Bert, Alan and the two Freds – did not seem to play doubles regularly and they were all much better than I. When I did occasionally play doubles with them after the Over-45s group on Mondays I found that I was by far the weakest player, which tended to produce a rather unbalanced match. It seemed much wiser to stay with my 'tennis ladies' as long as they could fit me into their group and to try to work on my game in this less pressurised setting. And, they were very nice people with whom I was slowly becoming reasonably friendly.

It is now summer vacation and I am trying to develop a game plan for doubles as I used to do and still do for singles. The first thing that I am going to do is to try to cover the centre of the court more aggressively when I am at the net and with a devil-may-care attitude and worry less about my side line. And, to improve my volleying at the net I am just going to get accustomed to using the chopper grip on my forehand and backhand or find a suitable alternative. I've noticed that several of the ladies seem to play at the net using their forehand grip while holding their racket so that the hitting surface is parallel to the net and to cover their backhand side as best they can with this same forehand side of the racket, rather than rotating the racket to its backhand side. I may not be seeing this correctly, but it seems to give them more time to prepare for a volley return as they do not have to rotate their racket, although it limits their ability to reach something hit to their far backhand. I think that I also will experiment with this approach.

And, in returning serves and during rallies, I am going to try to go down the side line more frequently. It helps me to have outlined a general strategy like this before a match as I find that there are so many things to think about once a match begins one can easily forget the basic points of your game that you would like to be working on.

I'm really hoping that I will be able to re-integrate myself into the weekly 'hit' with the 'tennis ladies' as they provide the right level of competition and a pleasant ambiance within which to play. However, I am concerned that my being a man might become a bit of an impediment both with respect to the tennis and also, more importantly, with respect to the chatter which goes on among them. Following my back surgery I was advised to take up Pilates, which I did over the following two years, at the same time that I started to play tennis. I was either the only male or one of two males in the several classes that I attended. I was the only male in the last class that I attended, which was made up of women who had been doing Pilates for a number of years. It became quite awkward for me to be in this class of all women, not so much because I was uncomfortable, but because I felt that my presence made the otherwise all-female class uncomfortable. I am a bit fearful that the same will happen with my 'tennis ladies'. I hope not, but if so then I guess that I will be off to social doubles!

CHAPTER TEN

How Old Was He?

My wife Jenny was always more interested than I in whether I had won or lost when I played a match. This was particularly true when I started to play in the mini-league for in the run up to playing I would usually refer to these as 'matches' rather than saying that I was going to have a 'hit' with Mike or with Sam. As soon as I would enter the door after the match Jenny would ask me "How did you do?" with a bright inquisitive look that gave away her desire to be able to drop the fact to her many friends and her serious tennis-playing 46-year-old son and his competitive tennis-playing wife – both of whom are captains of their club tennis teams – that I had won my mini-league match today or yesterday or whenever.

Unfortunately for my tennis-playing estimation in the eyes of my somewhat status-oriented and non-tennis-playing or sporty at all wife, I tended to lose slightly, or significantly, more matches than I won, depending on the division that I was in at the moment. So, it quickly became necessary to establish the approximate age of my opponents in order to redeem my 72-year-old self in the eyes of my wife who is the mother of the son and daughter-in-law who are both highly-ranked players in their club.

I knew that virtually all of my mini-league opponents were younger than me and that I had soundly beaten the two that I played against who were slightly older than me, one 11-0, But, it now seemed that I would have to get somewhat more precise ages as I was frequently being beaten by women players in my various divisions. It is more than a bit awkward to ask people their ages, especially women, but I did establish the fact that most of the people to whom I was losing in the mini-league were in their 30s and 40s, although I suspect that there may have been a few in their early 50s, and they were all much more experienced than I.

That does not mean that there are not people in the 60s and possibly even 70s in the higher levels (lower division numbers) of the mini-league. Mike is 67 and he is eight divisions higher (lower numbers) in the mini-league, and Paul is probably 60 or so and is seven divisions higher than I, and George is 65 and is a division or two above me. And Alan is certainly in his 60s and is around Division 15 when he plays in the mini-league. And I see many good players on the courts who must be in the 60s and probably even their 70s.

Nevertheless, most of the people to whom I lose when I play in the mini-league are 20 to 40-years younger than I who are either experienced players who are just not that good so they are in the same division as me, or younger players who only have been playing a bit longer than myself. This fact seems to have satisfied my wife so that given her need to chatter about all subjects on the telephone she can now add the caveat that "Yes, he also played today, but lost; however, he was playing someone who was only about 40"!

The approximate age of my opponents is also

important to me as I am constantly searching for a rough yardstick for how I am progressing in the sport. I don't mind losing to someone in their 60s or even early 70s if they are clearly experienced players who have been playing all of their life. Similarly, I don't mind losing to someone in their 30s or 40s or 50s who are experienced and are good players or who are clearly athletic and fairly good players even if they are not all that experienced. But, I like to be able to prevail against the mediocre players, like myself, and of whatever age, whether they are experienced or are only at or slightly above my level of experience. I have a self-concept of myself as being athletic and my ability to master tennis, even at my age, challenges that self-concept. Plateauing out and not improving my singles game beyond a certain point would tend to confirm for me the fact that I am ageing – which is something that I think that I am trying to counteract by devoting myself to tennis.

All this does not mean that I am impervious to the fact of age. I can play an 11-game mini-league match without being noticeably fatigued although, as noted earlier, my game might tail off a bit in the course of the match if I do not have at least a day of rest without playing tennis or jogging before the match. But, I do often have a problem with some of the younger 30 and 40-year-old male players who cover the court very well. I have lost to Ed, who is probably in his late 30s or early 40s, about five different times. In my estimation his game is only a bit stronger than mine, but he covers the court very well. I find that it is quite difficult for me to get the ball passed him and when he comes to the net and I successfully lob the ball over his head he is frequently able to return my lobs. It was in a match with Ed that I decided that rather than try to lob over the head of someone aggressively coming to the net I am better off trying to drive it far to their backhand side and just take the chance that they will not be able to reach it and volley it down my throat!

CHAPTER ELEVEN

Where Do I Stand Now?

Most of this book has been written during the summer of 2014 and as of today I have not played any tennis for about seven weeks, I was away on holiday for a while, then developed an arthritic big toe on my right foot that was quite painful and which did not allow me to engage in any physical activity. So, I used the occasion to write the first portion of this work.

I am quite out of shape as I have not had any exercise beyond the walking that one does as a visitor to hill towns in southwest France and a few one-hour-a-day walks about three-times a week over the past two weeks as my toe began to improve. I am enrolled in the mini-league session that ends after the first week of September and I have four matches to fit in by then. Not too many people are around as it is the end of the summer, and I don't want to exhaust myself or injure my toe by playing a rigorous two sets with Mike, if he is here.

Jenny's 44-year-old younger son is coming today with two of her granddaughters, and I hope that we will be able to have a hit either today or tomorrow or on both days. He hadn't played for years, but took up tennis again about two years ago and now plays regularly. He hits the ball quite hard and is becoming much more consistent than when I first played with him about a year-and-a-half ago, so I should get a good workout. I'll see how I feel after playing with him today, probably ok and just a bit stiff. I'll try to schedule a few friendlies in the next week and then I'll just play my mini-league matches and do the best that I can. I think most of the people in my current division are stronger players than I am, but if I can win four games in each match and maybe poach a win in one I will be more than happy.

CHAPTER TWELVE

Me

Academic Life and Marriage in the U.S.

I have told you about how retirement and ageing can leave gaps in your life and how taking up tennis as a 70-year-old helped fill in those gaps. And, of course, I have tried to convey to you some of the challenges that I have faced when I began to play tennis as an older person and my particular take on playing the game. At this point I think that it would be useful if I told you more about myself so that you can see how tennis fit into my life and what my needs were later in life that has led me to say that in some way I have been "Saved By Tennis".

As I write this I am now 73.62 years-old and have been playing tennis for 2.5 years. Pardon the decimal points, but it just struck me that their use in this manner is a bit idiosyncratic and I am nothing if not a bit idiosyncratic. I was an academic for over 30-years of my life and retired in 2002. My doctorate was in biological anthropology and I ended my career at a university on the east coast of the U.S. as chairman of my academic department and director of an interdisciplinary program and with the rank of professor emeritus. I was well-known in my field and had published a number of books and many articles and had been editor of a scientific journal and on the editorial board of another journal.

I wouldn't say that I was entirely pleased with my academic career. I had five children in the course of two marriages and both of my spouses only took short periods of time off from work after each child, so I had quite a bit of children-related responsibilities over the years. This made it somewhat difficult to totally devote myself to my work, and my second wife threated me with divorce if I were to continue to work so hard.

Other things also had an impact on my academic career. I was a product of the free-flowing lifestyle of the late 1960s and early 1970s which led to a number of relationships with women that were interesting and that enriched my personal life, but which distracted me somewhat from completely immersing myself in my academic pursuits. A much greater impediment to academic fulfilment was the highly corrosive effect of academic politics in my particular department and in the university. Marxist/Stalinist wannabees, strident feminism, political correctness and the appearance of racial and gay politics, the politics of academic promotion, and the presence in my department of several colleagues with what I can only charitably call severe character disorders and psychopathic tendencies made life in academia less pleasant than I had hoped for, particularly toward the end of my career. Suffice it to say that although I enjoyed teaching and doing my research, I was not particularly happy with my work situation.

Furthermore, neither of my first two marriages were particularly successful. So, as I glided into my sixth decade of life in 2000 I found myself in a second less-than-happy marriage that did not have much to draw us together as the three children of that marriage were now all out of the house and in university, and with a work situation that had progressed from unpleasant to intolerable despite the fact that I was chair and most senior person in my department. I take most of the responsibility for the failure of my second marriage, and I suppose that I could have been more effective in dealing with some of the problems that I faced in my academic setting; however, those are both rather charitable statements. As I rolled into my 60s both my marriage and my work situation were not at all good. On the surface everything looked fine to an outsider on both accounts, but beneath the surface, inside, I was a very unhappy puppy. My former wife Ann and I trudged along in our mutually unhappy marriage thinking only about the effect of a divorce on the kids, and I trudged along in my soul-destroying work situation. My sole form of relaxation was jogging, which I enjoyed along the lanes and byways of the beautiful New England town in which we lived, but jogging was a solitary activity, almost a form of meditation. I wasn't running competitively, or striving for anything in my jogging, or engaged in an activity that was different and challenging in its requirement that I learn a whole new way of doing something.

When I first looked at the system-wide email on January 2, 2002 announcing a fiscally-driven early retirement offer I didn't pay much attention to it. I had planned to work until I was about 70 as American universities cannot force faculty into retirement on the basis of age. Although I was not happy at work, three of my main antagonists in my department had previously announced their intentions to retire at the end of the academic year and I imagined that would make academic life more pleasant for me and that I would continue on as chair of my department or perhaps drift into some position in the administration.

However, I did look into this early retirement offer as I had a 70-year-old colleague who was considering retirement and I wanted to see if I could negotiate an additional financial incentive that would allow her to take up this offer. In discussing my colleague's situation and my proposals about some extra funds for her with Human Resources I was surprised to find that the senior HR person with whom I was dealing was going to take advantage of this offer herself and that she was younger than I and had fewer 'years of service' than I.

This led me to re-consider the offer with respect to myself. It was a good deal and there were significant financial incentives. Did I really want to continue being around these hypocrites and worse in this soul-destroying academic department and university for another 10-years or so? Did I really want to move away from teaching and research and become part of the dreaded administration for five to ten-years of my life? What would be left of me at the end of all this? I would have had a certain amount of additional status and power and my final salary pension would certainly have been higher, but what would be left of my individuality? And upon my eventual retirement, would I have the time and energy to enjoy life a bit while I still had my health and my mind was still relatively clear, or would I tumble out into retirement in 10-years with my mind even more glazed over and in the cookie cutter shape of a corporate clog?

I spoke with Ann and she graciously supported

my decision to take early retirement. She was four-years younger than I and she loved her work and expected to go on to 70, if not indefinitely. Therefore, it was economically possible to consider the offer. Thus, on June 12th in 2002 I entered the world of retirement. I remember still writing emails for two days after that date working out the details of the additional funds for my 70-year-old colleague, who sensibly also had decided to retire. Then, after that, my university obligations just came to an end.

In the months before retirement I had set up a website and was planning to do consulting work in my areas of academic interest – international nutrition and in genetic factors associated with resistance to malaria. However, I was absolutely drained from my last few months at the university as, in addition to my own work, I had to preside over the search for and hiring of two new faculty members and a reorganization of the status, terms of employment and benefits for all of our part-time faculty. Therefore, I decided to take the summer off and to start my consulting career in September. My daughter had recently finished university and was about to begin a one-year teaching/community outreach internship in a rural part of the state before going on to graduate school on the west coast and she needed some help moving and setting up her apartment. And, my wife's family owned an old farmhouse and 131 acres of land in a beautiful part of far northeastern Vermont. I was hoping that I would be able to unwind by chain sawing fallen trees and doing a bit of land management in that lovely setting. Little did I suspect what was coming my way!

To make a very long and complicated story short and uncomplicated, some serious problems arose in our marriage and in September 2002 we decided on a separation. Therefore, at sixty-two years-of-age I was faced with the prospect of leaving my very pleasant home on an acre of land in an equally pleasant community with its many acres of common land and nestled along the banks of an adjacent river for the unknowns of an apartment in a nearby city. My previous marriage had broken up in similar circumstances and I wound up leaving our lovely house in a nice neighbourhood for a roach-infested student dig on the somewhat trendy end of nowhere.

The prospect of life on my own had some appeal, but was really not that appetising. When I was on sabbatical in England in 1991/92 I had become friendly with a woman named Jenny and with her husband and several years later I heard that her husband had passed away. I had subsequently run into Jenny from time to time as I passed through on my way to Italy where I was doing some work and we had become good friends and had kept in regular contact. However, by September 2002 I had not seen or spoken to her for two years. Nevertheless, I was able to contact Jenny and we decided that she would come over to the U.S. for two-weeks and that we would see how we got along. That visit worked out quite well and Jenny returned to home to consult her kitchen cabinet of female friends and to ponder the prospect of us having a future together. We eventually agreed that I would come over permanently, so I picked up whatever possessions were worth/affordable bringing and arrived there to begin a new life in the

U.K. on December 17, 2002.

I had spent a sabbatical year in England in 1991/92, so it was not exactly *terra incognita*. But, I now found myself there at 63-years-of-age: having recently retired; being separated from my wife of 28-years and on the way to being divorced; living in the U.K. while all of my five children were in the U.S.; having rather fraught relations with my former colleagues in England over several issues; not being able to remember my way around anyplace outside of the university quarter of the city; having to deal with driving on the wrong side of the road and negotiating idiosyncratic British road layouts and traffic signalling systems and the extremely narrow streets usually accompanied by a woman who was a very confident driver but a person who was neither particularly good at giving directions nor distinguishing left from right when she did so; having to face a dreaded road test to acquire a U.K. driver's license; and having to deal with Ann's sense of hurt because I had moved so far away and the hurt on the part of several of my children as a consequence of the separation and the implied divorce, but more importantly because of the distance of my separation from them. And, of course, there was my enormous sense of loss of my home and family and proximity of my children as well as my effective disconnection from the university where I had spent most of my professional life.

Jenny and I got along very well and following my divorce from Ann we were married a year later in the U.S. at the home of a friend. All of my children and both of Jenny's sons attended and all of my children came to visit us in the U.K. in the first year, except my eldest son who has two children and heavy work obligations.

Retirement in England

This is the way my life in the U.K. began. There was some thought that I might find something to do at the University, but I wasn't interested in a full-time academic position and even a part-time position did not interest me as I had so many things to sort out in the course of settling in – visas, tax status, driver's license, as well as my family issues that were always just over the horizon, so to speak. Anyway, my relations with my former department in England were no longer amiable, so that probably would not have been an option even if I had wanted it. Some other possibilities in the University seemed to exist as well as an administrative position elsewhere, but I did not want to be working 60-hours a week or more and having to travel all over the world. Therefore, within my first year in England I discarded the idea of working within the University, or in any other academic setting, and began to settle into a less hectic life that would allow me to relax a bit, travel as much as possible, and get to know my new wife.

Jenny has a nice two-storey house with a lovely and relatively large 180 x 50 foot garden. I had had an acre of land at my house in New England and I always wished that I would have the time and mental space to devote myself to it more fully. I now had the time and increasingly had the mental space and Jenny's garden had need of someone to devote himself to it. Therefore, in the spring of 2003 I turned my attention to the garden and gardening became a major focus during my first few years in England.

Gardening

The climate in Britain is much more temperate than the climate in New England with its severely cold winters, short gardening season, and relatively hot summers. And, everyone in the U.K. has a garden. Houses almost invariably have flowers in front and in the garden at the rear -- usually a mixture of herbaceous perennials, shrubs, roses, climbers and with a sprinkling of annuals and trees and surrounded by hedges. Some people have small vegetable gardens as well, but that is a bit less common and not as iconic as the classic British cottage garden.

Everyone, especially women, are particularly knowledgeable about plants and gardening. To know your plants and to be able to talk about gardening is almost a sign, or insignia, of being an educated and proper person of a certain age. The local folk wisdom is that in a survey or middle-aged married English women, 40 percent or so preferred to do gardening than have sex.

There are many places open to the public in the U.K. where you can see truly exquisite gardens. The National Trust and the organisation English Heritage together have hundreds of properties many of which have gardens that are both lovely and unique. In the city where I live the various colleges that comprise the University all have charming gardens and these are usually open to the general public, at least on some occasions. And, there are innumerable gardens in front of houses on many streets that provide a free glimpse of the gardening and artistic bents of ordinary householders. There are also many private houses that periodically open their gardens to the public. And, there is the excellent University Botanic Garden with its vast collection of well-labelled and well-organised plants and trees.

So, there was no dearth of places from where I could get ideas about types of plants and gardening design and I made great use of the University Botanic Garden, the gardens at a number of the National Trust properties that we visited, the gardens at several of the larger colleges at the University, and the gardens of our many friends and acquaintances to develop my own sense of what I wanted to create in our garden.

Jenny's house is a two-storey brick house that was built in the 1920s along with several others to provide housing for married fellows at one of the colleges. The south-facing garden is about 180-feet long and about 50-feet wide and its bottom abuts the edge of the University Farm. It is a rather large garden by city standards. The fact that it borders on a portion of the University Farm, which is usually planted in grain, creates a rather peaceful setting.

Jenny has been in the house since 1975, but the rear garden, and the much smaller one around the car park in the front, required quite a bit of attention, which she did not have the time to devote to it until her retirement in 1997. Even then, being on her own and having a large house to take care of, as well as her various charitable activities, the garden did not receive as much care as it required. However, early in 2002, in the course of renovating part of the upstairs, she decided to make some changes to the garden and with the help of a landscape architect/gardener she established it in its current form.

The house has a small breakfast room with a table that seats four which we use for all meals except when we are entertaining five or more people when we would then use the dining room. This breakfast room addition is on the west end of the rear of the house and extends about 15 feet beyond the rear wall of the original house. As part of her 2002 renovation they constructed a 15-feet x 15-feet wooden deck along the side of this breakfast room extension that runs outside the dining room, and to the east of this she added a rather substantial 10-foot x 20-foot pergola which is behind the lounge. Slate flagstones were put in beneath the pergola.

The roughly 180-foot length of the garden extending to the south is divided in half by a well-establish 12-foot high yew hedge that has a six-foot wide break in the middle that forms the entrance to the lower half of the garden. There is a well-establish 10-foot high beech hedge that runs the full-length of the east side of the garden and an equally well-established, but somewhat wild-growing, lonicera hedge that forms the length of the western border of the garden. Jenny's landscaping work in early 2002 was limited to the first, or upper, half of the garden and the bulk of my efforts beginning, in spring 2003, were devoted to rescuing the lower half which was quite wild and a bit of a tip. I'll describe the entire garden to you so that you will have a sense of what was to become the major focus of my retirement activity beginning in the spring of 2003.

Looking at the back of the house from the upper garden you would see the breakfast room extending out about 15-feet on the left (west) side of the house with a sliding door from it leading into the wooden deck which is located in front of the dining room. Jenny had a fairly well-established wisteria growing on the south-facing wall of the house and a newly established, in 2003, purple clematis as well. A swing door opens out of the west side of the breakfast room beneath a clear plastic-roofed side passageway that proceeds around the breakfast room and onto a slate flagstone walk connecting to the pergola with its slate flagstone floor. The first garden beds are located between the flagstone walk and the end of the breakfast room and are planted in both red and white cystis, old fashioned roses, Michaelmas daisies, and several small bushes of uncertain identity. There is a rather large weigela in a bed on the far side of the walk and a rampant climbing rose that comes over from our neighbours to the west which creates a rather overgrown and flowery entrance to the garden from the side passageway that comes from the front of the house.

Three steps come down from the middle of the deck leading to the flagstone path and into the upper garden. To the left of the steps is another bed with more cystis and some choisya. The pergola is quite large, about 10-feet wide and extending about 20-feet from the door of the living room to the flagstone path at the start of the garden. Its four columns of double five-inch x two-inch boards on each side rise to about twelve feet above the flagstone floor and connect to single five-inch x two-inch boards that forms the upper frame and which connect to their parallel column on the other side. Although my experience with pergolas is not extensive, my sense is that this is a rather substantial-looking pergola.

On the western side of the pergola Jenny had a grape vine growing up the furthest column near the flagstone walk, followed by an Albertine climbing rose on the next column, another grape vine on the third, and then a portion of the wisteria from the south wall of the house going up the last column and onto the pergola. On the far, eastern, side of the pergola she had clematis on the first and second columns, a honeysuckle on the third, and a Philadelphus next to the fourth column. The grape vines became well-established over the years and covered most of the pergola as did the wisteria if it was permitted to do so, while the rose and the clematises provide some colour and variety. I planted some yellow winter jasmine on two of the far columns to provide us with a bit of colour at a time of year when there was not much else around.

The lawn extends for about 90 feet from the flagstone walk to the yew hedge at the end of the upper garden, and in her 2002 landscaping her gardener had created 10-foot wide beds on each side, with the one on the west, near the lonicera hedge, undulating, and the one on the east, near the beech hedge, straight. In the bed on the west side, near the property line, is a 60-foot or so hawthorn tree that has a mat of white blossoms in the spring and a bit further down toward the yew hedge is a rowan (mountain ash) tree of similar size which also has white spring blossoms. Half-way to the yew hedge on the east side, right on the property line, is a beech which now must be nearly 100-feet tall and which in addition to providing a perching place for a multitude of pigeons also provides a framework for the acrobatic squirrels to leap across the garden from beech to rowan – which we have the pleasure of viewing from our upper story bedroom window during the mornings while we sit in bed and sip our 'bed tea'.

The gardener put in a nice variety of choisya, buddleia, viburnum, peonies, cornus and bottle-brush hebes in the undulating west border with an edge of bergenia throughout. I added a bit here and there, mainly several large clumps of red tulips to provide early spring colour, several clumps of euphorbia, some Croscosmia lucifer (Moutbretia) which I transplanted from the bottom of the lower garden, and some campanulas which I am afraid were not particularly successful. In an attempt to get more year-round and some additional summer colour, this year I added euonymous, perovskia, several foxglove, and a large clump of red valerian.

Over the years I have done quite a bit on the east border, near the beech hedge, which really was quite under planted. Early on I transplanted some Bear's Britches (Acanthus), which a neighbour kindly game me, to provide some architectural effect, and after visiting one of the National Trust properties I planted a row of Rubus cockburnianus for its white bark for winter colour and several clumps of Cornus alba for its bright red bark colour during the winter and Cornus Winterfire for its bright orange winter bark colour. I have also scattered some red tulips and Croscosmia lucifer between the very tall beech hedge and the shorter and more straggly clumps of cornus and rubus. For some early yellow spring colour I have also placed several bunches of kerria along this border and I have recently added a clump of white valerian near the pergola. This border is also edged with bergenia. A nice Japanese Acer palmatum in a large clay pot in front of the yew hedge on the east side is also my touch and provides a dab of bright red throughout the summer.

Despite the fact that I have added quite a few plants to the upper garden I generally think of it as being the work of Jenny and her gardener – with its dramatic pergola, high hedges, and well-established shrubs. It is the lower garden that I consider to be my own and it was here that I allowed my imagination to run wild. When I arrived in late 2002 the lower garden was pretty much of a mess. Jenny and the gardener did not do anything with it in their 2002 landscaping project, so it was all mine. Unlike the upper garden, the lower garden does not have a central lawn. At our request, Jenny's elder son and his wife gave us a half-life-size faux marble statue of Venus with apple that stands on a pedestal which we placed in the gap in the yew hedge which leads to a central grass path between what I will call a 'wild garden' on the east near the beech hedge and a Gertrude Jekyll inspired 'sunken garden' on the west near the lonicera hedge. The 'wild garden' is a patch about 20-feet wide and 75-feet in length and the 'sunken garden' is approximately the same size. At the end of the grass path is another somewhat wild area I will call the 'bottom garden' and which is roughly 15-feet in depth and extends across the length of the property from the lonicera hedge to the beech hedge and along the property line with the University Farm.

The 'wild garden' has an eating apple and a cooking apple tree in its midst with a small pear tree between them. It is covered in green, but that was mostly ground elder. However, it was full of various kinds of yellow daffodils which made a brilliant show early in spring, but nothing thereafter. The 'sunken garden' was in an even sorrier state, but had lots of potential character. There was a central mound about 15-feet in diameter and surrounded by paths overgrown in weeds and overhung by a magnificent weeping willow on our neighbour-to-the-west's property. There had been a large conifer near the edge of the mound which Jenny had taken down, leaving a somewhat picturesque stump.

My work in Jenny's garden really began in the summer of 2003 on the mound area of the sunken garden. The first things that I did was to take the many chunks of irregularly-shaped limestone that were scattered in the sunken garden and arrange them around its borders, I then went to work on the mound itself, which rises about four-feet above the level of the paths in the sunken garden. I removed the weeds from the mound and planted a purple flowering bottle-brush hebe on the summit and four pittosporum with variegated leaves on its southern slope. There were lots of grape hyacinths on the mound as well as some aguilegia (columbines) and the overall effect was quite pleasant and not too fussy, and provided some colour on the mound throughout the summer. Jenny and I then laboriously removed the weeds from the path around the mound, put down a fabric base to prevent additional weeds growing through, and then with great effort covered the path with white gravel that we had delivered to our front car park and which we painfully carried to the sunken garden in a wheelbarrow.

I then planted an arc of hebe on the north edge of the mound extending along the central grass path toward the bottom of the garden so that as a person enters the lower garden through the gap in the yew hedge and past the statue of Venus with apple he would encounter a three-foot high bank of hebe stretching around the front of the sunken garden and along the grass path toward the bottom garden. At a point where a small mungho pine bush makes a break in the hebe is an entrance to the path around the mound and into the sunken garden. A friend had given us some small bare-rooted red roses for an anniversary present early in our marriage and I planted them beyond the hebe. Over the years they have grown extensively and provide a large brilliant cluster of red half-way down the central grass path.

I have also added a very spindly and twisting cotinus in a triangular area in the sunken garden next to the grass path going down the centre of the lower garden and this provides an interesting architectural form and dark reddish colour, although it requires constant pruning to prevent it from blocking the path. I also have put in some interesting small sedum and semper vivum in this triangle along with a juniper edging around its border. Another little patch on the edge of the sunken garden has a cluster of red valerian and in the bottom of the sunken garden is a large clay pot with a pieris.

A series of severe frosts during the winter of 2011 devastated my beloved mound, killing off the then very large bottle-brush hebe and the very lovely pittosporum and making the mound look bare again. Another purple bottle brush hebe has finally become well-established over the past three years and I have added some prostrate euphorbia, which I particularly like, and a low-growing green and white variegated plant that looks a bit like the pittosporum, but which is more like high ground cover than trees. Additionally, I have circled the hebe at the crest of the mound with five escallonia bushes which have a pretty pink flower but which are taking a while to become well-established. The loss of the large hebe and the pittosporum was a big setback for me, but I learned that if there is diversity in the garden there will always be areas that are looking nice.

I have also done quite a bit in the wild garden, perhaps actually more than anywhere else. I planted a climbing pink/red rose and a large number of Lysimachia punctata in the middle of the wild garden after having seen them in our friend Paul's excellent cottage garden, and they provide nice yellow colour throughout the summer. I also put in a yellow cytisus (broom) in the wild garden just beyond the yew hedge and the Venus statue and this gives nice architectural form and a bright yellow colour in spring, and I have a very large patch of Bear's Britches (Acanthus) near the beech hedge toward the middle of the wild garden. I also have several patches of red Penstemon garnet along the back of the wild garden near the beech hedge, although these have not held up well over the years and have required some reinforcements. As an alternative to the Penstemon I put in some fuchsia near the beech hedge as well. I like Verbascum olympicum, which grows to about six-feet in height, so I always plant a few in the wild garden; however, I only have had sporadic, if somewhat dramatic, success with them. Three patches of purple loosestrife are also quite lovely as are a line of Verbena bonariensis and some sedum along the front border of the wild garden next to the path. A new pink and white laventera provides colour near the yew hedge along with a large patch of brilliant purple Michaelmas daisies and two weigelas, which I recently planted, are just getting started near the second apple tree.

I have planted a line of thuja and cupressus at the back of the bottom garden to provide a screen against the large housing development that the University will be building on the farm within the next few years, and I have allowed the bramble to go up in height as well. I put what is now a lovely Korean dogwood in this area, a small variegated cornus which has delicate blossoms in the spring, and a purple hibiscus. There is also a mass of large deep-red Croscosmia lucifer at the bottom as well as a good sprinkling of the smaller orange form. We also have quite a few day lilies and irises in this area and an occasional foxglove. For winter colour, I planted four light green cupressus toward the front of the bottom garden amongst the other plants. These would grow into trees, but I top them off at a height of about three-feet every few years and maintain them as four distinct bushes.

So, you can see that gardening became a significant focus of my life in retirement in England. Among the things that I did, gardening probably occupied a greater percentage of my time and my thoughts than any other activity from spring 2003 to about the summer of 2008, and it still fills much of my time and that of my wife, although it is increasingly more of an maintenance activity, Outside my relationship with my wife, I would say that gardening has provided me with more pleasure than any other activity, even travel – which is a bit ephemeral – and is certainly my most creative form of expression. I enjoyed jogging, but I did that mainly for health reasons and at a leisurely pace that was almost like a form of meditation.

I was a bit surprised to see how I took to gardening when I arrived in England as I really did not devote much time to it when I lived in the U.S. There, most of my effort was directed to planting trees and I ceded all authority and interest in our small cottage/kitchen garden to my former wife Ann. A clue to my interests in landscaping or gardening may come from when I was a youth of around eight to fourteen-years-of-age. I had two ten-gallon tanks with tropical fish and enjoyed, particularly when I was younger, watching the fish and especially watching the guppies and black mollies bear their offspring. However, as I became older what I particularly enjoyed doing was planting up my aquarium with different plants and placing unusual things like carrots and stalks of celery upright in the sand in some sort of Dali-esk stance. My father thought that I was bonkers, but I believe that were the seeds of my gardening interests.

The Residents' Association

Although it had begun a few years earlier, by 2006 it became clear that the University intended to develop the approximately 300 acres of the nearby farm, including the portion of it behind our house, for housing and other university purposes. This obviously caused us great concern as it would be occurring right at the base of our garden and would replace a quiet and picturesque field of grain with an uncertain amount of development. There was, and still is, a significant housing shortage in the city and it appeared to us that the planners on the City Council envisioned a rather dense development to help them solve these housing needs. In 2006, in order to confront the development of this site I, working with some of my neighbours, founded a residents' association which we called STOPIT. To make things manageable and to enable us to primarily look after our very local interests, we limited membership to those houses bordering the field just behind us. From 2006 to 2012 we, mainly myself, engaged in innumerable discussions with the University's development office and later with members of the planning department at the City Council. During this period of time, particularly early on, we participated in several public consultations and wrote detailed official and individual representations to each. We eventually convinced the University and City Council to agree that the housing behind our gardens would be single-family, detached houses that were no taller than the 10-metre height of our houses and which had 20-metre gardens backing onto our gardens. They further agreed that tallest buildings would be located toward the centre of the site far away from us and that the highest buildings in the centre of the field behind our houses would be three or four-storeys.

Being trained as an anthropologist I have a long-term interest in community development and since the anti-Vietnam war movement of the late 1960s I have had a commitment to participatory democracy. So, the idea of a neighbourhood residents' association (RA) was natural. Moreover, since moving into Jenny's house in I had been surprised at how people along her street did not know one another, being acquainted with perhaps their neighbour on each side of their house and that is about all. However, given the common threat of a vast development at the base of our gardens, all except one household agreed to join STOPIT. We acted collectively and had a board which I led for the first few years. This activity took up a fair amount of my time between about 2006 and 2010, but it was rewarding to see that we were able to enter into an effective dialogue with the University and reach a mutually satisfying agreement. I gave up the role as lead in 2010 and dropped out of the board itself a year later after the basic outlines of the development had been established and after several members of the board became more engaged in the daily running of the RA. I wanted STOPIT to have a breadth of leadership so that it could sustain itself over the years and not have it dependent on a single person, myself.

My activities in founding and participating in the running of STOPIT became a major focus of my life in England between 2006 and 2010. In addition to the various development issues, I had instituted an annual summer party which took place in the garden of a different house each June or July and that contributed significantly to a growth of a sense of community in the neighbourhood. People actually began to get to know one another and to talk to one another. However, the business of STOPIT, if one were to do one's job properly, was basically confrontational –whether it was with the developers who were trying to purchase adjacent houses in order to demolish them and build a block of flats, or the City with its various proposals and its desire for denser development, and even the University, although we had developed an excellent working relationship with them, And, I was becoming tired of this responsibility while others seemed to be grasping for it and for the opportunity it offered them to interact and be known by the local politicians, planners, and the development officers at the University.

Self-publishing and ebooks

One of the main reason for my taking a secondary role in STOPIT was that I was becoming interested in trying my hand at creative writing and self-publishing. I had published a number of scholarly books and scientific papers and was the editor-in-chief of a scholarly journal for a number of years, but I really wanted to see what it was like to write a non-scholarly work, especially a work of fiction. Amazon had recently created a paperback self-publishing facility as well as a facility to publish ebooks on their Kindle reader and Barnes & Noble and other publishers had done the same. I wanted to write something that would please myself and see whether it would fly, and did not want to go through the lengthy and uncertain process of submitting my work to standard publishers.

Although I am a biological anthropologist professionally, I have also been trained as a cultural anthropologist and have spent much of my adult life doing my own ethnography of everyday life in my head. I am particularly attracted to humorous satire of aspects of contemporary life, and as a 73-year-old person I have lived through a variety of cultural changes in the U.S. and have had 12-years of field experience in Britain. Therefore, between gardening, and STOPIT and jogging, and shopping, and cooking and cleaning, and making my wife Jenny and myself 'bed tea' in the morning, and dealing with my five children in the U.S. and their various issues, I began to write contemporary satire which I self-published through Amazon under a pseudonym.

It was fun to write this work, more or less like doing a Jackson Pollock painting compared to the factual precision of a scholarly work in my field. Through my characters I could say whatever I liked to say about whatever aspect of social life that I wanted to say it about. And since I was doing this for fun and had no literary reputation to make or defend, I could do it in an individualistic way that was an expression of myself, and not something confined to the requirements of a particular genre, or publisher, or editor, or readership; and if no one read the books I would have had the pleasure of having written them and could place them in that proverbial chest in the attic to be discovered after my demise by some inquisitive child or grandchild!

Once written, the process of formatting the text in the proper manner for Amazon's self-publication process is confusing , but there are a number of people who can do this for you for a very modest fee and Amazon provides a list of reliable formatters, However, publishing something is only the first part of the process and marketing your book and getting it known from among the tens or hundreds of thousands of books that are being self-published is another issue. Enter Twitter, Facebook and various other despicable forms of social media. I won't say how many tweets my anonymous author has made or how many people he 'follows' and, more importantly, how many 'followers' he has. But, I will say that I did not enjoy this process and spent too much time reading and sending too many zany and newsworthy tweets.

Although I am extremely pleased with my self-published books, and my eldest son described my initial satire as a 'work of genius', I am sorry to report that these works have not been overwhelmingly popular or overwhelming financially successful. I spent a good few years working on that project and it was fun. And, it led me to think that perhaps I should do something to which a greater number of people could relate. Which brings me here, trying to talk to you about how there can be a loss of your major focus when you retire, how it feels as you become older, and how tennis has now provided me with and important year-round focus to take up that space, in addition to my beloved gardening.

CHAPTER THIRTEEN

Saved By Tennis

I have told you about how retirement has created a bit of a void for me to fill and I am sure that many readers may have had the same experience – initial jubilation and sense of freedom for being off the treadmill, followed by a spate of traveling, followed by devoting yourself to one activity or another, followed by some health issues affecting you and/or your partner, followed by a slight disconnection between you and your partner as both of you age and no longer have the presence of the children or grandchildren to bind you together, followed by a further disconnection between you and your partner as sexual interest or ability wanes and that activity is no longer as binding as it was in the past, followed by throwing oneself compulsively into one activity or another just to take up your time, and perhaps followed by a bit of a let-down or hollowing out or depression as you sense that you just have a finite amount of time on this planet and that you are losing both your physical and mental powers and that you have not done anything new over the past few years or mastered something that you had done less well.

I think that you can see from my story how this played out in my life. Raising five children was pretty much of a full-time job over a period of almost thirty years. There almost always were one or two young people in the house and just having to deal with their presence and various school and social issues was enough to keep anyone engaged. And then there was work with its constant real and less real demands: preparing your lectures; getting to know and advising students and dealing with their various problems; writing grant applications and administering grants; doing your research and writing papers; getting the papers which have been submitted to your journal reviewed and corresponding with the authors, and reading papers sent by other journals to you for you to review; organising conferences and going to meetings and conferences; dealing with department issues such as student complaints about poor teaching or sexual harassment; dealing with a nasty departmental secretary who cannot be fired; allocating merit pay increases within your department; dealing with university issues; and being up and out of the house at 7 am and commuting an hour each way back and forth to work, among other things. All this may lead you to feel frantic and stressed-out, but you are too busy to wonder about what you will be doing with your free time and even if you cannot think of new scholarly challenges or directions the system will spit up new challenges that you will be required to deal with and the big bureaucracy of work, especially in academia, will always have some committee or some teaching initiative or some computer literacy program for you to get involved in.

But, when you retire that all comes to an abrupt end. Period. And that is the absolute pleasure of retirement and I have cherished every minute of my retirement and could not conceive of going back to work again, even part time. However, again, after the initial jubilation you have to have something to do in life. When I was working I never had time to read a not-work-related book nor did I ever read a newspaper or watch television. We went out to dinner on occasion, socialised on occasion, and went to the occasional play, concert or ballet. Now, in my retirement I make 'bed tea' for my wife and myself when we awake and we lie in bed listening to the morning news on Radio 4 and spend some time with one another within the limits of our current interests and capacities, and we have a leisurely breakfast of porridge followed by all-bran flakes to further insure that our digestive systems will function perfectly. And I have time for a leisurely shower and time to scrape the water off the glass surrounding the shower and wipe it off the fixtures as instructed. And after breakfast I have time to floss my teeth carefully with dental tape, clean them for at least one and hopefully two full minutes with my electric toothbrush and my low-priced sensitive-teeth tooth paste, and then gargle for at least 30-seconds with my Listerine Freshburst mouthwash. And I carefully make the bed while continuing to listen to the news, unless it is more than usually repetitive, fluffing the pillows and placing Jenny's nice cotton nightgown which I bought for her between her two-pillows then fluffing the duvet and carefully putting it beneath the fluffed pillows at the top of the bed, and then carefully putting the bedspread on top of the duvet while making sure that it is not pulled down too far so that it will not cover the already-fluffed pillows and making sure that it is not too long on the outer traffic-side of the bed so that I will not trip over it.

My current morning ritual could take me to 9 or

9:30 am. When I was working it was up and a quick wash, something quick for me and the kids to eat, get them out for the 7:05 school bus, quick brush of teeth in about 15-seconds, forget the bed and get out and into the car for the life or death battle with the SUVs and pick-up trucks on the way to work. And one did not have to wonder what one would be doing that day, especially if it was raining and you were not able to go into the garden!

Well, what does one do next? Jenny always had a routine of household tasks. The calendar blocks are turned as soon as she comes downstairs in the morning and the breakfast dishes are promptly removed from the breakfast table, rinsed and put into the dishwasher. And then the clothes and towels are washed and when they are finished they are always hung on the outside clothes drying apparatus even in the middle of winter or when there is an 80 percent probability of rain, and when the laundry finally is dried she will laboriously but gleefully iron everything, including my shirts – which I always sent to the dry cleaners when I was working. And there are always other tasks to do like siliconing the shower, grouting the shower tiles, and adding more gravel to the already well-gravelled front car parking area.

Jenny comes from Lancashire and at heart she is her mother's daughter and a 'Lancashire housewife'. Everything is organised. She will begin with cooking the dinner meal, not every morning but on some mornings. That might involve a complex soup like minestrone with lots of chopping, or a courgette (zucchini) and lemon soup that requires careful and slow preparation, followed by a main dish like a tagine that requires lots of peeling and chopping and cooking, or aubergine (eggplant) parmagiana with its lengthy cutting and frying, or a vegetable bake with cheddar cheese with its lengthy period of sautéing and stirring the vegetables, or roast leg of lamb with roast potatoes and carrots and parsnips on weekends, and innumerable coulisses from our blackberries and red currents and her many complex desserts.

And Jenny spends much more time in the garden than I do. She has removed every dandelion that has ever appeared on our rather large lawn, flower beds, and wild garden and has done a pretty good job on the other infiltrants, including moss. And she is most feared by nettles, ground elder, rampant rose of sharon and other enemies of orderliness. While I favour the overgrown look, Jenny will hack away at our many disorderly and semi-wild bushes and is quite excellent in getting things into our compost bins and turning them on occasion, which I tend to forget to do.

However, what takes up even more of Jenny's time, or more generously put, what she devotes much of her time to, are her various charity involvements. When she was in employment Jenny had been a social work manager for the County Council and as a consequence of that work she had become a founding member of three charities: one which provides housing for elderly people and which recently built a 76-unit 'complete care' retirement home just outside the city; another which built and runs a retirement home for elderly Vietnamese people; and a third that provides services to people with disability. Being on the boards of these charities involves regular meetings and frequent telephone conversations, thus, her involvement with them fills up a significant part of Jenny's time – almost like work, and in a way that my life is not filled up.

Besides her charity-related frequent and lengthy telephone conversations, Jenny spends ages on the phone talking to everyone under the sun, but especially to her three close female university friends and a number of other, mainly female, friends, as well as to her younger son who lives in London and who has two young daughters and is faced with complicated childcare needs as he frequently travels abroad for work and because his wife works in Geneva, Switzerland. And Jenny has a niece (actually a more complicated relationship than that) with whom she burns up the telephone lines when she calls her or receives a call from her. But what is most striking to me is how Jenny sometimes goes from one telephone call to another and how lengthy each call can become.

In contrast, I am reasonably tidy, but avoid constant cleaning and straightening up, especially since we have two cleaners who come in for an hour-and-a-half weekly and there are only two of us at home. And Jenny thankfully has the monopoly on the laundry, although I will occasionally hang it out and/or take it in, being quite attentive, as directed, to whether it begins to rain. Although I prepare about a third of our dinners I usually do them in about thirty minutes plus five minutes for Jenny's almost-nightly gin and tonic, so it does not really take up that much of my time. And, although my famous pasta sauce takes a good one-and-a-half-hours to prepare, I only do it about once every three weeks. And my share of preparing our porridge every morning and peeling the skin off of the half of an apple that goes into Jenny's porridge is also not that time consuming.

Though I spend a fair amount of time in the garden, sometimes as much as five hours at a stretch, it is usually in spring when I am undertaking a planting program or in autumn when I am putting the garden to bed, and never because I am just looking for something to do. But the main activity that Jenny has that keeps her busy is her three charities and I have not flowed into something like that from work nor have I taken up charity work on retirement, unlike a friend of ours who recently retired and who spends a full-day each week working for the Citizen's Advice Bureau and also sings in a men's choir! Unfortunately, charity work has not appealed to me and I doubt that I would be permitted to open my mouth in any choir – male, female, or mixed!

Furthermore, I have not lived here for the greater part of my life and I do not have the broad network of friends and work connections with whom I can chatter incessantly on the telephone and with whom I can get together on a fairly regular basis for lunch, or coffee, or tea, or shopping. And I do not go to get my hair done every few weeks or so as Jenny cuts mine, as well as my beard, every third week as I sit on the stool in the bathroom in my blue boxer shorts, which are only used on that occasion, nor do I regularly visit the Vietnamese nail parlour to have my toe nails cut and painted – at least without being well-disguised. And, I do not do the Guardian crossword puzzle every day!

Moreover, my children all live in the U.S. and are quite involved in their own lives and not particularly involved with mine, although I do skype with the eldest of my three sons and his family every other week. Ironically, I am getting the same cordial disengagement from my five children that I gave my parents once I left the family home for university and then proceeded into the world of graduate school, employment and family life. Nothing hostile, but very little connection. Therefore, I am not constantly on the telephone or penning off emails to my children as I have painfully learned that they are not, so to speak, dying to hear from me.

So, here I am in merry old England at 73-years-of-age: fully retired from my academic position and with little interest in engaging with my generally pompous and self-important academic colleagues; out of regular contact with my family; having done as much traveling to the continent, Asia, North Africa as I am interested in doing for the moment as I do not want to travel continuously just to keep busy and our budget and Jenny's obligations to do grandchild care for her four six-to-ten-year-old granddaughters will permit; having my garden largely planted-out and moving more into a maintenance phase of that noble endeavour; having shot my wad with the residents' association; having tried my hand at Kafkaesque satires of contemporary life; and finding that after my spinal surgery and my wife's chemotherapy for lymphoma three years ago, and with our incremental movement into our seventh-decade of life, we both seem somewhat less inclined to chase one another around the bedroom or tumble out of the shower on top of one another when the shower door gives way under the pressure of our two pulsating bodies.

I attended a Spanish conversation group for a

few years and I will be beginning a French conversation group this autumn, and Jenny and I chatter a bit in French at home. She is reasonably fluent as she spent a number of summers in the southwest of France as a teenager with the family of her French exchange friend Nicole, while I only have spent about a month in France every other year or so since we have been married and I have been in Britain. But, for me the French conversation group is work, not a pleasure; something that I subject myself to rather than something I approach with a smile.

In steps tennis! It just hits the spot for me. Chess doesn't and rambling is nice but doesn't cut the same mustard. I now only jog for a mile or two weekly and always on the cushioned surface of the University track, so jogging is no longer central to my life, and I find long cycle trips boring except on rare occasions. I attend one chamber music concert weekly and another one monthly, but that, although satisfying, does not make me smile and it immerses me in the same old para-university group of people, not the mix of people I encounter at tennis.

I am athletic and I enjoy playing tennis. I find it a bit frustrating in that my game is not as good as I want it to be, and I am frustrated that I did not start playing earlier in life and continue throughout my life so that I would now play with the developing ease that Jenny's 10-year-old granddaughter shows after playing for two years of fairly intensive tennis training under the auspices of her long-time tennis-playing mother. But, I am where I am. If I had been playing all of my life it might not have been as much interest to me now as it is since I have been trying to pick it up from scratch at this late date. If I had been playing all of my life I might not have had anything to strive for. I certainly would not have had to learn the rules of tennis and to have figured out, as best I could, the basic strategy of the game. I wouldn't have any excuse for playing the way I play since I would have been playing my entire life. Perhaps as an experienced player I would feel more pressure to win my matches rather than just playing to enjoy myself. And I doubt that I would be finding that I learn something new in every match, from playing every player I play, especially those who are a bit, but not overwhelmingly, better than I am. Would playing as an experienced player give me as much to strive for as I now get out of tennis, or would it just be something that I do, like going to a concert or going on a seven-mile walk?

I think that it is the element of learning something new that has made tennis so attractive to me at this point in my life. It is like improving my spoken French, but it is more fun. There is a great sense of accomplishment in both, but the element of physical exercise makes tennis that much more enjoyable to me and the pleasure of playing outdoors is almost as good as the seven-mile ramble. It is a particular pleasure to play in the morning at 8:30 when the air is crisp and the sun is low in the sky and when the courts are empty and all that you hear is the additional delight of the chirping of the birds.

I am sure that it is the element of learning something new coupled with the fact that I find it to be an enjoyable game which can be played outdoors that has made tennis so attractive to me. And another plus has been that through the Over-45s group and the mini-league I have had the opportunity to meet a variety of different people. I think that I would have enjoyed devoting myself to improving my chess playing abilities, and I could have become involved in the process to the point where I would have been seeing chessboards and chess strategies in my mind as I lay in bed on the way to sleep rather than tennis balls zooming at me or opportunities for drop shots or backhand returns down the line. But, chess lacks the physical exercise of tennis and sitting indoors gazing intently at a chessboard is not quite the same as ranging around a tennis court with the trees and the birds as a backdrop and bathed by the sun and touched by a hopefully gentle breeze.

I would have liked to learn to play the cello, but the necessity of dealing with the expectations of a teacher did not appeal to me, particularly when most teachers are probably more accustomed to coaching younger pupils who, because of the greater plasticity of their youthful brains, are more likely to learn to play in the manner that their teacher would like them to play, compared to a 73-year-old relic who has difficulty remembering the name of a plant that is called 'orchid'. And, again, there is a different kind of physical activity in music than in tennis and not much connection to the outdoors, although I suppose that one could regularly practice and play *en plein aire*.

Skiing is quite enjoyable, but if you haven't learned to ski by 70-years-of-age it is probably worthwhile giving that activity a miss. Anyway, the spinal fusion in my neck had put an end to my skiing career! And cycling, while a great passion of many, including older people, and a wonderful form of exercise and an outdoor activity as well, is just not for me. Too monotonous, and who wants to be driving on the roads with all of those cars or in the cycle lanes with the lycra-clad brigade zooming past you? Although I am certain that there is much to learn about the art of cycling, it doesn't seem to be the same type of learning that goes into making you a tennis player and then a better tennis player! The 15-minute cycle ride to and from tennis three or four times a week and the occasional cycle ride into town are enough for me.

Woodworking, or collecting antiques, or joining an investment club, or volunteering at a National Trust property, or volunteering at the Citizens Advice Bureau may all be worthy endeavours but would not have filled the hole for me. Tennis has, and in doing so I feel that I truly can say that I have been 'Saved By Tennis'.

CHAPTER FOURTEEN

August/September 2014

I wrote the first draft of this book during the summer of 2014. We had been away in France for a while and I had not had the chance to play tennis for about six weeks although I had, with hopeful expectation, brought my racket and some balls with me. Upon our return a somewhat arthritic big toe on my right foot acted up and I was in some pain and was taking strong anti-inflammatory medication and was not able to play for a further two weeks during August. However, I was in the August mini-league session and had several matches scheduled for late August and early September which I approached with some trepidation as I had not had any time to practice because of my injured toe. I think that I'll end by telling you a bit more about my tennis activities during the past month so that you can see where I now am in the sport and how I am dealing with the continuing challenges that tennis presents to me.

Mini-league

Henry, my opponent in my first match in late August, was someone who had just moved back to the city and was re-entering the mini-league. He was a nice chap of about 60 to 65 years-of-age who was semi-retired and who had been playing tennis for many years. He was obviously a better tennis player than I, but not overwhelmingly so. His serve was more consistent and had some speed to it, but it was not that difficult to handle and he tended to predictably send it down the middle of the court. He had a good forehand and a serviceable backhand. And, because he has played quite a bit of doubles he was extremely good at volleying (hitting the ball in the air before it bounces) from all positions on the court, including some excellent backhand volleys of my returns rather deep in the corner.

My serve was rusty and I double-faulted much more than usual, probably because I had decided that I would not let up too much on my second serve and I lost the match 9-2, which is a pretty good thrashing. Yet, I enjoyed every moment of the match and learned quite a bit about playing against someone like him. And it was a beautiful morning, a bit crisp at first but with a bright sun in the sky and a fresh smell to the morning air. And despite my loss I was looking forward to my next match the following Saturday against a thirty-something young lady who recently beat Henry 6-5 and to whom I have lost the four or five matches that we have played over the past six months or so. It is because of this joy and anticipation and pleasure that has been added to my life that I feel that I truly can say, as before, that I have been 'Saved By Tennis'.

I actually beat Betty, the thirty-something young lady, 6-5. I played very well and hit the ball as hard as I could and deep to her backhand as often as I could, with some success. I didn't double fault much and I held up well under pressure, winning the match in the final tie-break game. I think that the secret of my success here was that I hit the ball hard throughout the match and didn't become conservative when I was ahead. I was now one and one in this mini-league session and had high hopes for my remaining matches.

My third match was with Ted, a 44-year-old fellow (we discussed our respective ages), who has been playing for about six years. He was a left-handed player and I thought that I would have considerable success against him as one of my better serves curves in rather sharply to the backhand of a left-hander and I thought that I also would do well against his backhand in my ground game. The first two games went to deuce multiple times, but I lost them both and eventually lost the match 9-2, although it was much more competitive than the score indicated. I served well and did not double fault at all, but he was very good at covering the court and I just could not get it passed him. I then went for the corners and lost a number of points by a few inches. Despite the decisive loss it was a very pleasant game played on a lovely day and, again, I think that I learned quite a bit in the process.

My fourth, and final, mini-league match in the August session was against Janice, who was probably in her late 40s. She was an experienced player who had just re-entered the mini-league competition after having been out for a while. When we warmed up she looked steady, but not intimidating, and I thought that I had a good chance against her. Unfortunately, I did not play well and I lost 8-3. There was just something missing in my game. I didn't hit the ball as hard as I could and after fluffing a drop shot attempt by hitting it too high I neglected that option, which probably would have been effective against her. Her ground game was steady and she just let me make the unforced errors that characterise my game. Nevertheless, it was an enjoyable match despite the fact that I was somewhat disappointed by my lacklustre performance.

My record in the August mini-league session was one victory and three defeats (1-3). I am not entirely sure how it was figured, but Ted went up a division (lower number) Betty and Henry stayed at the same level, and Janice and I went down one division (higher number). Because one player in the September session has dropped out due to work conflicts, I only had three matches in that session – Rita, Janice again, and my mate Alice who has moved up from a lower division.

Rita was my first match in the September session. She is Ted's wife and probably in her early 40s. I had played her previously about a year ago and had won. Our paths diverged as I drifted up into the higher divisions (lower numbers) and she stayed about at the same level, but over the past few sessions I have been on my way down and she has been on the way up. I arrived for our match a bit early and a friend with whom I was chatting said that Rita has been having regular coaching and was now a much stronger player. That proved to be true as she beat me 8-3. I didn't play all that poorly, but made too many unforced errors and hit too many of my returns just a bit long. I just had my racket re-strung in mid-August, so I think the problem is me and not my racket being too loose. As I began to hit long I slowed down the velocity of my returns which gave her medium speed returns that were frequently right up the middle. The one time she came to the net on a shot to my backhand I tried to wham it past her to her backhand. I got good velocity on the shot, but it was too close to her and she was able to kill me with a good backhand volley. I could easily have lobbed it over her head, but I have been following my anti-lob strategy which unfortunately was not successful here – I should have pulled it further away. Rita is an experienced player who is quite steady. She had me running quite a bit from side to side and I was surprised at how I fluffed many returns that were deep to my forehand and in the corner, but were returnable. I don't think that I was setting my feet very well and probably should have chosen to make defensive deep lobs rather than trying to put so much velocity on the ball. My serve was not great, but is becoming a bit steadier. I did change the pace and placement of my serve better in this match, but also double faulted about three or so times. I was disappointed to have lost to someone I had beaten, but, as usual, I learned quite a bit about my game, and from watching Rita play, and was pleased with the success of several of my drop shots.

My second match in the September mini-league session was with Janice, the person who I had lost to 8-3 in the August session. I was well-rested, not having played for three days prior to our match, so I was certainly not fatigued. I was terrible in the first two games and could not get anything over the net and she took a 2-0 lead. But I came back and tied it 2-2 and then we went to 3-3. She went ahead 4-3, then 5-3, then 6-3 before I came back to win the last two games – ending in a 6-5 loss for me. I didn't play badly, except for the first two games when I just didn't seem able to get started. My serve was good and improved during the course of the match and I was hitting the ball fairly hard on my returns. And, I used my drop shot effectively on several occasions. But, in addition to a fair number of unforced errors I made a number of mistakes on several key plays. On two occasions I dashed in for relatively easy returns close to the net with most of the court open to me only to hit the ball wide. I was right to go to the side of the court, but should have been aiming for the side third of the court, not the side line. On another occasion my drop shot from up close was more of a pop-up, which she returned to my disadvantage, whereas I could easily have powered it straight down the line. And, on two crucial occasions I stuck with my anti-lob strategy when she came to the net only to hit two good returns a bit too close to her backhand; on both occasions I could easily have lobbed it over her head! However, I played fairly well and we had some very long rallies, most of which I lost. Janice is an experienced player who is not overpowering, but quite steady and very court-savvy. However, if I am ever going to move up the ladder I will have to stop making so many unforced errors and poor shot choices!

After having improved my performance in my second match with Janice, and after having had three or four weeks of coaching with Tim, I had high expectations of myself in my next mini-league match with my buddy Alice. Alice had lost her first two matches this session against Janice and Rita, as had I, and by slightly greater margins. My match with Alice started out well as I won the first game and was up 40-15 in the second game. I then botched a few easy returns and lost the second game and went on to lose the match 7-4. For whatever reasons, I just played terribly. My serve was ok and I did not double fault at all, but the rest of my game was dreadful. I hit innumerable returns of moderately-paced serves into the net and my ground game was just as bad. I just couldn't seem to put any velocity on the ball and when I did I drove it into the net. In my coaching session with Tim the day before, he advised me to step into the ball and push off on my rear foot as I hit it. I think that I may have been concentrating too much on my footwork and not concentrating on hitting the ball squarely with my racket – as whatever I was doing led to a subpar performance, even for me. Or, perhaps I was a bit tired at my advanced age after having had such a rigorous, non-stop hitting session with Tim the day before. What bothered me most about this defeat was that perhaps 60 percent or more of the points that I lost were due to completely unforced errors on easy shots. Alice did not play poorly, but I really defeated myself. It was a bad way to end this mini-league session and a downbeat note on which to end my description of my progress in the world of tennis to you in this book. But, at about 53-years-of-age Alice is 20-years younger than me and she has been playing tennis on and off all of her life and has had regular coaching with Tim over the course of the past four years. And, more importantly than winning, we had an enjoyable match between good friends on the empty courts of the Club at 8:30 in the morning in a light mist and with warmish weather on the second of October and with the occasional chirps of the birds to keep us company. What else could I ask for? Furthermore, I have a singles friendly scheduled tomorrow morning with

Jake, a very pleasant chap from the Over-45s whose play is more or less at my level, and Alice and I have agreed to get together for a friendly sometime next week.

Doubles with the tennis ladies

The first time that I played doubles with the tennis ladies in late August I had a terrible time with my serve and with my playing in general. We were using brand new club balls and I was hitting everything long. I had lost my touch, if I had ever had it, over the six or seven week period when I had not played and I was having trouble getting it back. In contrast, they had been playing quite a bit over the summer and were much better tuned than I. The subsequent few weeks has seen some improvement on my part in my weekly session with the tennis ladies. I played with them on the afternoon after I had lost to Rita in the mini-league in the morning and my serve was much improved. I am also becoming much better at the net than I was and am covering the centre of the court much better. I have also become better in dealing with the opposing net player and now do not hesitate to go down the side line in returning a serve or a groundstroke or attempt to go over the head of the net player without fearing that I will hit it long.

Mike and Bert and another chap in his 60s and a young man in his 20s arrived to play doubles one afternoon in late September while I was playing doubles with the tennis ladies. I felt a bit self-conscious that I was playing with the ladies while two of the better male players from the Over-45s group, Mike and Bert, were playing in an all-men's group. But, that is where I am in my tennis development, still somewhat of a novice, especially at doubles, and I am probably seven to ten years older than either of them. And, I am beginning to hold my own against them in the Over-45s, especially in the singles competitions!

More coaching with Tim

As I said previously, I had some coaching with Tim over a period of three months about a year-and-a-half ago and had found it quite useful, but stopped because I felt that I needed more competitive match experience. My singles friendlies and my playing in the mini-league have given me that experience and I now find that it would be useful to get more 'hitting' practice with Tim and additional coaching to help me with some areas of my game that need particular improvement. And, I noticed that Alice, who has been having coaching with Tim for about four years, and Mike, who now has had coaching with one of the women coaches for about two years, have both improved considerably. Therefore, I made arrangements with Tim for a one-hour per week coaching session for Wednesday mornings at 10:30.

I have mentioned before that my games tend to have relatively short rallies – maybe six to ten returns or less – so I don't get that much practice 'hitting' when I play competitively. In contrast, my hour with Tim is almost continuous rallying so I have an opportunity to get a lot of hitting repetitions under his watchful eye. Because my backhand is much weaker than my forehand return, we concentrated on that part of my game.

Our sessions start with a bit of warm up and then full-court rallying both forehand and backhand. Tim knows that I want to work on my backhand so he makes sure that he hits it there regularly and he gives me pointers as we proceed – about six basic points (if I have remembered them correctly). First, that I use a proper backhand grip and have my racket turned to the side well before the ball arrives. Second, that I position my racket at my waist level, rather than at the level of my shoulder where I have tended to place it, as I prepare to make a backhand return. Third, that I turn my shoulder further to the side so that I get more swing from my body rotation on my backhand returns. Fourth, that I step into the ball as I swing. Fifth, that I make sure that I carry my swing forward and up, instead of straight forward. And sixth, that, if possible, I do not swing above shoulder level on high-bouncing balls to my backhand, but position myself appropriately and wait for the ball to fall below shoulder level. I have heard this all before from my beginner's class. But now that I am a somewhat more experienced player it is very useful to have Tim remind me about these points and for him to assess the degree to which I do them on each return.

Another thing that I wanted to work on with Tim is my return of slow serves and slowly-paced ground strokes. I'm reasonably adept, for my level of play, at returning moderate to strong serves and getting a good velocity on my returns, and the same with a strong ground stroke. Using the velocity at which they arrive I am able to generate a pretty strong reply myself. But, when I receive a slow serve, usually a second serve or a serve of one of the women players who does not have a strong serve, I often have a problem generating as much pace on my return as I would like. If I swing hard, to get speed on my return, I have a tendency to hit the ball long – often just beyond the baseline. If I take a more moderate swing so as to assure that I do not hit the ball long, I tend to produce a return that lacks the pace that I want.

Tim observed that I appear to be aiming too high when I return a slow ball and suggested that I aim my returns at three levels depending on where I am on the court. He suggested that if I am between the service line and the net when I take a slowly-hit ball, I should aim to hit it just over the net and not at head height where I seemed to be directing these returns. He suggested that I aim for head height when I am between the service line and the baseline, and that when I am behind the baseline I should go for 'fence height', the height of the fences at both ends of the court. I have put this advice to the test and it generally seems to work. When I come up close to the net to hit a weakly-hit ball I really must keep my return low of I will bam it beyond the baseline; and when I retreat behind the baseline to return a lopping soft shot my tendency has been to aim my return at head height, which produces a return right down the middle of my opponent's court near the service line and sets them up for a strong reply. Aiming at 'fence height' seems to have helped me get my returns deeper in my opponent's court.

Another problem that Tim has helped me with is getting better angles on slowly paced balls that bounce in the vicinity of the service line. I usually try to angle the ball to the corner or side line with my wrist, but Tim has suggested that with a slowly moving ball I could do it more effectively if I would hit the ball earlier, when it is a tad in front of me, rather than waiting for it to arrive and trying to angle it solely with my wrist!

CHAPTER FIFTEEN

Adieu

You have now heard my story about taking up tennis from scratch as a 70-year-old. In telling it I hope that I was able to convey to you how I really feel that I have been SAVED BY TENNIS! A lot has to do with the circumstances of my life and I trust that you will pardon me for having gone into that in some detail. What was particular about my situation is that I retired precipitously and without any planning and then found myself in the process of a divorce and moving to England within a period of six months. Thus, I was completely disconnected from the home and community in which I had lived for the previous twenty-four years, my children, my friends and neighbours and my former workplace. And, after I decided not to follow any academic pursuits, I had scads of free time.

Most people transition into retirement more slowly and in a more stable situation with respect to their family connections and their ties to friends and community, but I was really quite adrift. Because I had not lived in England for sixteen years and had not maintained my professional connections, most of my socialising and friendships during my first few years in Britain were through my wife Jenny. And not having any avocation like tennis, or golf, or whatever, when I arrived left me without a vehicle for making connections with other people. I did join a Spanish conversation group at the local U3A early on and did develop some decent friendships there, but speaking Spanish, or French, or any language, although satisfying, does not put a smile on my face. It is a class that you attend once a week and have the pleasure of using the language when you are abroad, but that is it. Jenny doesn't speak Spanish so that we could not chatter at home. And I wasn't particularly interested in Spanish cultural events or going off to Spain all of the time, or purchasing a house in Spain – although we did consider it until we decided that we would rather buy something in southwestern France, if we would do something like that at all. However, being in our 60s and my having so many things to do to settle into the UK a house abroad was just not in the cards.

For the first years of our marriage Jenny was a non-executive director of a National Health Service Trust as well as being on the boards of her three charities. And her four granddaughters were coming along. So, she was a very busy bunny. I had my long-distance family issues to deal with, including various young-adult crises about university, graduate school and jobs as well as organising my banking arrangements and finances, passing the road test for a UK driver's license, getting my spousal and permanent visas and UK citizenship, doing most of our travel planning and making travel arrangements, and getting started with my work on the garden.

Therefore, at first, I had plenty of free time, but also quite a lot on my plate. If I already had been a proficient tennis player, I probably would have joined the Club and it would have been a good way for me to make a new set of friends. However, given that I did not play tennis at all I am certain that I would not have had the mental space to take on something completely new, like learning to play tennis, at that point in time when I had to contend with so many other new things – including a French conversation group in my attempt to improve my ability to chatter with Jenny in French at home.

However, after five years or so the banking and visa arrangements were sorted out and my children and my former wife in the U.S. settled into their own lives rather oblivious of me, and the garden became more developed and less demanding of my time, and after an enormous flurry of travelling we began to be a bit tired of that, and I had spent as much time as I wanted to spend on the residents' association and on my epublishing endeavours. Then I had my back problem and could only jog a bit, and I slowly began to have more and more free time with virtually nothing in particular to do. Jenny now had her four granddaughters, who became a major focus of her life and whose occasional grandchild care needs placed additional demands on her time. Then, Jenny developed lymphoma which was successfully treated with chemotherapy, but which slowed her down a bit in some ways.

Again, if I had been a proficient tennis player I would have joined the Club early on and playing tennis would have been a useful personal outlet for me – something that I could have done on my own, independently of Jenny. But, I didn't play tennis at all, so I did not have that outlet. However, things changed in 2011 after my spinal surgery and Jenny's diagnosis and successful treatment for lymphoma. I could no longer jog, but had a need for regular physical activity and an equally strong need to find a new set of social connections of my own. Cycling myself or in a group was not the answer nor was joining a rambling group with Jenny as I really wanted to do something that belonged to me. And working-out solitarily in a gym did not fit the bill. I had always wanted to play tennis and paradoxically had lived in a community of 104 houses for 24 years that that had three excellent tennis courts, and had regularly jogged past the Club here in England over the past 10 years. So, it was time to start on the path of being SAVED BY TENNIS.

I am actually just embarking on my journey into the world of tennis. It has been a wonderful experience finally learning to play and becoming somewhat proficient – probably like learning to sail. It is just great to get out on the court and have a hit and even better to be involved in a competitive friendly with someone you know and with whom you are compatible. It is actually exhilarating. And, it is a very portable game that you can play anywhere. I took my racket with me on our recent trip to the area around Cahors in southwestern France, but did not find the opportunity to use it. However, I do take my racket when we visit Jenny's competitive tennis-playing elder son and his even more competitive tennis-playing wife and I have played at their club, although they have not deigned to hit with me – assigning their 10-year-old daughter the task instead. But, I have hit with Jenny's younger son on vacation on several occasions and am hoping to be able to strut my stuff to her elder son and daughter-in-law before I am too arthritic to do so.

I also still have not availed myself of the many social dimensions of the Club. I have never attended any of the social doubles sessions primarily because I fear that people will assume that I am a better player than I am and put me in with a group that is too competitive for me. I don't mind playing a bit above my level, but it makes the match less enjoyable for the other players if I create a much weaker side. However, I am working on my doubles game with the 'tennis ladies' and I am rather sure that I will be ready to enter the major leagues by this coming summer!

The Club also has periodic tournaments which I could enter. One of the women from the Over-45s with whom I am friendly, who is not one of the 'tennis ladies', always remarks to me that we should have entered this or that mixed doubles tournament together as a team. But, again, I don't think that I am quite ready for tournaments, but have put it in the back of my mind as something that I might be keen on doing by next summer. There are actually many tournaments that come along that place you with three other players and then which pair you off with one another or in different teams, but my game will have to improve somewhat before I inflict myself on some of these serious players as a partner – hopefully, again, by this coming summer.

The Club also has a purely social dimension which I currently have not explored and know little about. The clubhouse is not fancy, like something you see at the local golf club, but is merely a large bungalow with a single large room and some changing and showering and storage areas. However, alcohol is served periodically – I believe after or during social doubles on Thursday evenings, and there seem to be frequent barbecue evenings and other evenings when food is served.

And, I vaguely remember seeing notices about live music in emails that come my way. There is also an annual dinner at a decent Italian restaurant in town, and there is a Wimbledon ticket draw that affords one the opportunity to get tickets to the Wimbledon Tournament, another activity I have not taken advantage of although I have attended Wimbledon independently on several occasions.

There are a number of inspirational aspects about playing tennis at the Club. I have mentioned watching some of the 10 and 12-year-olds who are just outstanding players and I remember being absolutely blown away, as they say, watching a 15-year-old young lady practicing backhand slams (yes slams, not volleys) on lobs hoisted up deep in her court by her father. But, what is most inspirational to me is to see the enthusiasm for tennis among some of the older players. One expects enthusiasm for sport in youth, but the enthusiasm and devotion to tennis that I see in some of the senior players is truly impressive.

I don't go to the Club on weekends when the very best senior players in their 40s and 50s, play. And I have never watched any of the Club teams practice or play and do not know who constitutes these teams, although that is also something I wish to pursue as I become more involved with the Club and as it becomes more of a nexus for part of my social life in the future.

However, what I especially enjoy is watching, out of the corner of my eye as I play with the 'tennis ladies' or during an afternoon friendly, a group of four chaps who are probably in their late 50s or early 60s who play doubles together almost every afternoon. There are probably about six of them, but two are real regulars. They are excellent players and what impresses me most is how often they play. They are just out there all of the time, drizzle or shine! They have obviously been playing all of their lives and although I am sure that there are younger players who are better than them it is a particular pleasure to watch them play. And, I really fervently wish that I could achieve their level of proficiency, although I am afraid that will have to wait for one of my future incarnations!

The other very inspirational group are two chaps who I believe are in their mid-80s who play singles against one another almost every morning and doubles with two other chaps as well. I don't know them very well, but I do chat with them a bit if we are playing on adjacent courts or when I arrive early for the Over-45s and they are the only players on the courts. They really go at it and are quite decent players, although their serves are not very strong and their ability to cover the court is somewhat limited. One of them told me that he had to teach the other to play tennis with his left arm some years ago after an undisclosed injury/medical event deprived him of the use of his right arm. It is particularly impressive to see the two of them all bundled up in heavy clothing in the middle of winter out on court number 1 at nine in the morning before anyone else has arrived!

So, learning to play tennis has opened up a whole new life for me. It is an enjoyable game played in a pleasant outdoor setting with a convivial group of people. And, while Jenny is counting on her crossword puzzles to ward off mental decrepitude, I am pleased to have found that I have been able to do a reasonable job getting a handle on the basics of the game of tennis, with respect to both my physical playing of the game and my grasp of some sense of the strategies involved in the game. I also have made some progress with my spoken French, but it is tennis which puts a bounce in my step, a gleam in my eye, and a smile on my face – a good reason at 74-years-of-age to say that I have been SAVED BY TENNIS!

Printed in Great Britain
by Amazon